DATE DUE

iLL 4/14

DEMCO, INC. 38-2931

Wired for Innovation

Wired for Innovation

How Information
Technology Is
Reshaping
the Economy

Erik Brynjolfsson and
Adam Saunders

The MIT Press
Cambridge, Massachusetts
London, England

For information about quantity discounts, email specialsales@mitpress.mit.edu.

Set in Palatino. Printed and bound in the United States of America.

Library of Congress Cataloging-in-Publication Data

Brynjolfsson, Erik.
Wired for innovation : how information technology is reshaping the economy / Erik Brynjolfsson and Adam Saunders.
    p. cm.
Includes bibliographical references and index.
ISBN 978-0-262-01366-6 (hardcover : alk. paper)
1. Technological innovations—Economic aspects. I. Saunders, Adam.
II. Title.
HC79.T4.B79 2009
303.48'33—dc22

                                                            2009013165

10 9 8 7 6 5 4 3 2

Contents

Acknowledgments

The idea for this book originated in a request by Michael LoBue of the Institute for Innovation and Information Productivity for an accessible overview of research and open issues in the areas of IT innovation and productivity. With guidance and inspiration from Karen Sobel Lojeski at the IIIP, and through the IIIP's research sponsorship of the MIT Center for Digital Business, we were able to devote more than a year to studying the main research results in these areas and to producing a report that eventually became this book.

We are also grateful to the National Science Foundation, which provided partial support for Erik Brynjolfsson (grant IIS-0085725), and to the other research sponsors of the MIT Center for Digital Business, including BT, Cisco Systems, CSK, France Telecom, General Motors, Google, Hewlett-Packard, Hitachi, Liberty Mutual, McKinsey, Oracle, SAP, Suruga Bank, and the University of Lecce. We thank Paul Bethge and Jane Macdonald at the MIT

Press for their editing and for expert assistance with the publication process. Heekyung Kim, Andrea Meyer, Dana Meyer, Craig Samuel, and Irina Starikova commented on drafts of portions of the manuscript.

The ideas, examples, and concepts discussed in the book were inspired over a period of years by numerous stimulating conversations with our colleagues at MIT and in the broader academic and business communities. In particular, we'd like to thank Masahiro Aozono, Chris Beveridge, John Chambers, Robert Gordon, Lorin Hitt, Paul Hofmann, Dale Jorgenson, Henning Kagermann, David Verrill, and Taku Tamura for sharing insights and suggestions. Most of all, we would like to thank Martha Pavlakis and Galit Sarfaty for their steadfast support and encouragement.

Introduction

The fundamentals of the world economy point to continued innovation in technology through the booms and busts of the financial markets and of business investment. Gordon Moore predicted in 1965 that the number of transistors that could be placed on a microchip would double every year. (Later he revised his prediction to every two years.) That prediction, which became known as Moore's Law, has held for four decades. Furthermore, businesses have not even exploited the full potential of existing technologies. We contend that even if all technological progress were to stop tomorrow, businesses could create decades' worth of IT-enabled organizational innovation using only today's technologies. Although some say that technology has matured and become commoditized in business, we see the technological "revolution" as just beginning. Our reading of the evidence suggests that the strategic value of technology to businesses is still increasing. For example, since the mid 1990s there has been a dramatic widening in the disparity in profits between the leading and lagging firms in industries that use technology intensively (as opposed to *producing* technology). Non-IT-intensive industries have not seen a comparable widening of the performance gap—an indication that deployment of technology can be an important differentiator of firms' strategies and their degrees of success.

Despite decades of high growth in investment, official measures of information technology suggest that it still accounts for a relatively small share of the US economy. Though roughly half of all investment in equipment by US businesses is in information-processing equipment and software (as has been the case since the late 1990s), less than 2 percent of the economy is dedicated to producing hardware and software. When the computer systems design and related services industry is added, as well as information industries such as publishing, motion picture and sound recording, broadcasting and telecommunications, and information and data processing services, the total value added amounts to less than 7 percent of the economy. However, when it comes to innovation the story is quite different: every year in the period 1995–2007, between 50 percent and 75 percent of venture capital went into the funding of companies in the IT-production and information industries. We also see much greater turbulence and volatility in the information industries, reflecting the gale of creative destruction that inevitably accompanies disruptive innovation. Firms in those industries have a much higher ratio of intangible assets to tangible ones. Because valuing intangibles is difficult, wealth for firms in these industries is often created or destroyed much more rapidly than for firms that are in the business of creating physical goods.

The literature on productivity points to a clear conclusion: information technology has been responsible, directly or indirectly, for most of the resurgence of productivity in the United States since 1995. Before 1995, decades of investment in information technology seemed to yield virtually no measurable overall productivity growth (an effect commonly referred to as the productivity paradox). After 1995, however, productivity increased from its long-term growth rate of 1.4 percent per year to an average of 2.6 percent per year until 2000. But information technology wasn't the sole cause of the increased growth. A significant body of research finds that the reason technology played a larger role in the acceleration of productivity in the United States than in other industrialized countries is that American firms adopted productivity-enhancing business practices along with their IT investments.

In the period 2001–2003, productivity growth accelerated to 3.6 percent per year, making that the best three-year period of productivity growth since 1963–1965. Whereas economists generally agree on the causes of the 1995–2000 productivity surge, there is less consensus in the literature about the 2001–2003 surge. We attribute it to the delayed effects of the huge investments in business processes that accompanied the large technology investments of the late 1990s. The literature suggests that it can take several years for the full effects of technology investments on productivity to be realized because of the resultant redesign of work processes. An ominous implication of this analysis is that the sharp decline in IT investment growth rates in 2001–2003 may have been responsible for the decline in measured productivity growth 3–4 years later. In 2004–2006, productivity growth averaged only 1.3 percent. However, in 2007 and 2008 productivity growth nearly returned to its 1996–2000 rate, approximately 2.4 percent per year. If our hypothesis is correct, this may have been due in part to an increase in investment in IT that began in 2004.

The companies with the highest returns on their technology investments did more than just buy technology; they invested in organizational capital to become digital organizations. Productivity studies at both the firm level and the establishment (or plant) level during the period 1995–2008 reveal that the firms that saw high returns on their technology investments were the same firms that adopted certain productivity-enhancing business practices. The literature points to incentive systems, training, and decentralized decision making as some of the practices most complementary to technology. Moreover, the right *combinations* of these practices are much more important than any of the individual practices. Copying any one practice may not be very difficult for a firm, but duplicating a competitor's success requires replicating a portfolio of interconnecting practices. Upsetting the balance in a company's particular combination of labor and capital investments, even slightly, can have large consequences for that company's output and productivity. As in a fine watch, the whole system may fail if even one small and seemingly unimportant piece is missing or flawed.

The unique combination of a firm's practices can be thought of as a kind of organizational capital. We are beginning to see in the literature the first attempts to value this intangible organizational capital, which could be worth trillions of dollars in the United States alone. Some researchers use financial markets, some attempt to add up spending on intangibles, and others use analysts' earning estimates to answer a basic question: How large are the annual investment and the total stock of intangible assets in the economy? For example, at the start of 2009 Google was worth approximately $100 billion but had only $5 billion in physical assets and about $18 billion in cash, investments, and receivables (according to balance-sheet information and financial-market data for December 31, 2008; total financial value is the sum of market capitalization and liabilities). The other $77 billion consisted of intangible assets that the market values but which are not directly observable on a balance sheet. Because the literature is not yet well developed, we expect to see more work in this area in the coming years. Various researchers have estimated that the annual investment in these intangibles held by US businesses is at least $1 trillion. A large portion of it does not show up in official measures of business investment. We see the attempt to quantify the value of these intangibles as a major research opportunity.

Producers of information goods face a major upheaval because of declining communication costs and because of the ease of replication and reproduction. Never before has it been so easy to make a perfect and nearly costless copy of an original information product. The music industry was one of the first to confront this transformation and is now going through a major restructuring. Many other industries will face similar disruption. An important task will be to improve the intellectual-property system to maximize total social welfare by encouraging innovation by producers while allowing as many people as possible to benefit from innovation at the lowest possible price.

Non-market transactions involving information goods generate significant value in the economy and provide a promising avenue for research. The total value that consumers get from Google or Yahoo searches is not counted in any official output statistics, and thus far no academic research has even attempted to quantify it. The lucrative business of keyword advertising pays for these searches. Internet users' demand for searches feeds the advertising market at search-engine sites and also drives visitors to publishers of other content. Highly targeted keyword advertising then feeds demand back to the advertisers' sites. The two sides of the market are mutually reinforcing, which makes keyword searches and keyword advertising an example of *information complements*. The makers of information complements may subsidize one side of the market to promote growth of the other, as in the case of Adobe giving away its Reader software to enlarge the market for its PDF-writing Acrobat software. The cumulative value of the free or subsidized halves of these two-sided markets is potentially enormous, but today we have no measure for it. And there are other business models—exemplified by Wikipedia, YouTube, and weblogs—that generate enormous quantities of free goods and services, accounting for an increasing share of value, if not dollar output, in the world economy.

There are no official measures of the value of product variety or of new goods, but recent research indicates that this uncounted value to consumers is tremendous. In this book we examine an additional metric not included in government accounts as an important method of measuring the effect of technology on the economy. This metric is *consumer surplus*. Although the idea of consumer surplus is more than 150 years old, the use of this methodology to empirically value the introduction of entirely new goods or to value changes in the variety, quality, and timeliness of existing goods is relatively recent. However, the uncounted value from information goods is simply too large to ignore, and we need to do a better job of measuring it.

Aspects of the information economy that couldn't be measured by traditional methods can now be measured, analyzed, and managed. We used to think that the intangible nature of knowledge and information goods would make it virtually impossible to measure productivity, because of the difficulties inherent in measuring knowledge as an input and as an output. In an information economy, can we actually measure how much value came out versus how much data went in? The problem is not that we don't have enough data—it's that we have too much data and we need to make sense of it. To that end, we are excited by the results being generated from the first attempts to use email, instant messaging, and devices that record GPS data to construct social networks. These studies are being conducted at what we like to call the "micro-micro level," the first "micro" referring to the short time period and the second to the unit of analysis. With such data now being generated in the economy, we may be better able to measure productivity than ever before.

Managers and policy makers can better understand the relationships among information technology, productivity, and innovation by understanding the insights offered in recent literature on these topics. In this book, we summarize the best available economic research in such a way that it can help executives and policy makers to make effective decisions. We examine official measures of the value and the productivity of technology, suggest alternative ways of measuring the economic value of technology, examine how technology may affect innovation, and discuss incentives for innovation in information goods. We conclude by recommending new ways to measure technological impacts and identifying frontier research opportunities.

Wired for Innovation

1   Technology, Innovation, and Productivity in the Information Age

In 1913, $403 was the average income per person in the United States, amounting to a little less than $35 a month.[1] To be sure, $403 went a lot further back then than it does today. A pack of cigarettes cost 15 cents, a bottle of Coca-Cola 5 cents, and a dozen eggs 50 cents. If you wanted to mail a letter, the stamp cost you only 2 cents. You could buy a motorcycle for $200. If you were wealthy, you could buy a new Reo automobile for $1,095, nearly three times the average person's annual income. The Dow Jones Industrial Average was below 80, and an ounce of gold was worth $20.67.

In 2008, the average income per person in the United States was $46,842—more than 115 times as much as in 1913.[2] At the end of 2008, a dozen eggs cost about $1.83,[3] a stamp was 42 cents, and the average price of a new car was $28,350.[4] The Dow Jones was above 8,700, and gold was about $884 an ounce.

How do we correct for the erosion in the value of the dollar created by more than 90 years of inflation? Typically, the federal government uses a monthly measure called the Consumer Price Index (CPI) to track changes in the prices of thousands of consumer goods, including eggs, stamps, and cigarettes. According to the Bureau of Labor Statistics, prices, on average, have increased by a factor of nearly 22 since 1913.[5] On the face of it, this means that it would cost 21.7 times $403, or about $8,745, to purchase in 2008 a basket of goods and services equivalent to what could have been bought for $403 in 1913.

But think of all of the products and services you use today that were not available at any price in 1913. The list would be far too long to print here. Suffice it to say that a 1913 Reo didn't come with power steering, power windows, air conditioning, anti-lock brakes, automatic transmission, or airbags. Measuring the average prices will give you some idea of the cost but not the quality of living in these different eras.

Why are so many more high-quality products available today? Why are we so much wealthier today than people were in 1913? The one-word answer is the most important determinant of a country's standard of living: productivity. Productivity is easy to define: It is simply the ratio of output to input. However, it can be very difficult to measure. Output includes not only the number of items produced but also their quality, fit, timeliness, and other tangible and intangible characteristics that create value for the consumer. Similarly, the denominator of the ratio (input) should adjust for labor quality, and when measuring multi-factor productivity the denominator should also adjust for other inputs such as capital.[6] Because capital inputs are often difficult to measure accurately, a commonly used measure of productivity is labor productivity, which is output per hour worked. Amusingly, while we live in the "information age," in many ways we have worse information about the nature of output and input than we did 50 years ago, when simpler commodities like steel and wheat were a greater share of the economy.

Productivity growth makes a worker's labor more valuable and makes the goods produced relatively less costly. Over time, what will separate the rich countries from the poor countries is their productivity growth. In standard growth accounting for countries, output growth is composed of two primary sources: growth of hours worked and productivity growth. For example, if productivity is growing at 2 percent per year and the population is growing at 1 percent per year,[7] total output will grow at about 3 percent per year.

When we talk about standard of living, output per person (or income per capita) is the most important metric. Total output is not as relevant. Here is why: Suppose productivity growth was 0 percent per year, and population growth went up to 2 percent. Then aggregate economic output would also grow at 2 percent if output per person remained the same. The extra output, on average, would be divided among the population. Thus, if a country wants to increase its standard of living, it has to increase its output per person. In the long run, the only way to do so is to increase productivity.

Even changes of tenths of a point per year in productivity growth could mean very large changes in quality of life when compounded over several decades. This leads to the question of how countries can achieve greater productivity growth. While the answer includes strong institutions, the rule of law, and investments in education, in this work we focus on two other major contributors to productivity improvements: technology and innovation.

Economists like to tell an old joke about a drunk who is crawling around on the ground under a lamppost at night. A passer-by asks the drunk what he is doing under the lamppost, and the drunk replies that he is looking for his keys. "Did you lose them under the lamppost?" asks the passer-by. "No, I lost them over there," says the drunk, pointing down the street, "but the light is better over here." In our view, this highlights an important risk in economic research on productivity. The temptation is to focus on relatively measurable sectors of the economy (such as manufacturing), and on tangible inputs and outputs, rather than on hard-to-measure but potentially more important sectors (such as services) and on intangible inputs and outputs. However, the effects of technology on productivity, innovation, economic growth, and consumer welfare go far beyond the easily measurable inputs and outputs. It may be clear that a new $5 million assembly line can crank out 8,000 widgets per day. But what is the value of the improved timeliness, product variety, and quality control that a new $5 million Enterprise Resource Planning (ERP) software implementation produces, and what is the cost of the organizational change needed to implement it?

We find that the most significant trend in the IT and productivity literature since 1995 is that it has been moving away from the old lamppost and looking for the keys where they had actually been dropped. Economists, rather than assume that technology is simply another type of ordinary capital investment, are increasingly trying to also measure other complementary investments to technology, such as training, consulting, testing, and process engineering. We also see better efforts to examine the value of product quality, timeliness, variety, convenience, and new products—factors that were often ignored in earlier calculations. But we still have a ways to go.

In the late 1990s, there was a financial bubble in the technology sector. One need not look further than the rise and fall of the NASDAQ index (figure 1.1), the rise and subsequent leveling off of the stock of computer assets in the economy (figure 1.2), or the decrease in the number of news stories about technology since 2001 (figure 1.3) to be lured into thinking that technology has reached the peak of its strategic value for businesses. In a provocative 2003 article that supports this philosophy, Nicholas Carr asserted that IT had reached the point of commoditization, and that the biggest risk to IT investment was

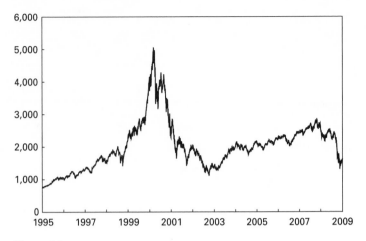

Figure 1.1
The NASDAQ index, 1995–2008. Source: Yahoo Finance.

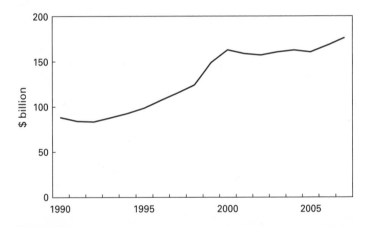

Figure 1.2
Current-cost net stock of computers and peripherals. Source: Bureau of Economic Analysis, Fixed Assets, table 2.1, "Current-Cost Net Stock of Private Fixed Assets, Equipment and Software, and Structures by Type," line 5. This refers to how much it would cost to replace computer equipment. For example, at the end of 1990 it would have cost $88 billion to replace all the computers held by business, in 1990 dollars, whereas at the end of 2007 it would have cost $176 billion in 2007 dollars to replace the computers in the economy.

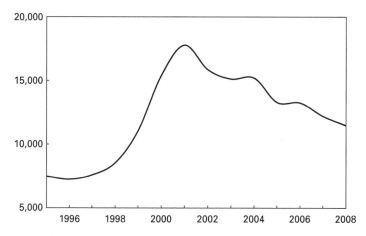

Figure 1.3
Number of stories mentioning "technology" in the *New York Times*, the *Wall Street Journal*, and the *Washington Post* combined. Source: Factiva.

overspending. "The opportunities for gaining IT-based advantages," Carr wrote, "are already dwindling. Best practices are now quickly built into software or otherwise replicated. And as for IT-spurred industry transformations, most of the ones that are going to happen have likely already happened or are in the process of happening. Industries and markets will continue to evolve, of course, and some will undergo fundamental changes. . . . While no one can say precisely when the buildout of an infrastructural technology has concluded, there are many signs that the IT buildout is much closer to its end than its beginning." (Carr 2003, p. 47) Carr concluded that companies should spend less on IT, and that technology should be a defensive investment, not an offensive one. His article resonated with many executives who had been lured in by the exuberance of the financial markets only to witness the subsequent destruction of trillions of dollars of market value.

However, we think that it was not the technology that was flawed, but that investors' projections of growth rates for emerging technologies were too optimistic. Some underlying trends in technology itself tell quite a different story. The real stock of computer hardware assets in the economy, adjusted for increasing quality and power, has continued to grow substantially (albeit at a slightly reduced pace since 2000). This adjusted quantity accounts for the increases in the "horsepower" of computing since 1990. As figure 1.4 shows, businesses held more than 30 times as much computing power at the end of 2007 as they did at the end of 1990.

Now consider innovation. As can be seen in figure 1.5, the number of annual patent applications in the United States has continued to grow steadily since 1996.

As we mentioned in the introduction, Gordon Moore predicted in 1965 that the number of transistors on microchips would double every year, and in 1975 he revised his prediction to every two years. What became known as Moore's Law has held for more than 40 years as if the financial bubbles and busts never occurred. In fact, according to data presented by the futurist Ray Kurzweil, if one goes back to the earliest days of

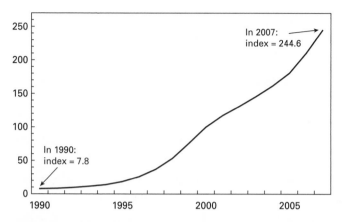

Figure 1.4
Quantity index of computer assets held by businesses in the U.S. economy, with year 2000 = 100. Source: Bureau of Economic Analysis. Fixed Assets table 2.2, "Chain-Type Quantity Indexes for Net Stock of Private Fixed Assets, Equipment and Software, and Structures by Type," line 5.

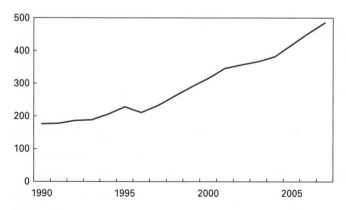

Figure 1.5
Total patent applications in the United States (thousands). Source: U.S. Patent and Trademark Office, Electronic Information Products Division Patent Technology Monitoring Branch (PTMB), "U.S. Patent Statistics Chart Calendar Years 1963–2007" (available at http://www.uspto .gov).

computers one can observe exponential growth in computing power for more than 100 years. Kurzweil also pres-
ents evidence demonstrating that over this longer time
period Moore's Law may have accelerated. (See figure 1.6.)
In figure 1.7, to put these changes into perspective, we offer
an example from Intel.

While Moore's Law has steadily continued over the
decades, 1995 marks a significant change in how IT could
be changing competition in the United States. Figure 1.8
illustrates the performance gap in IT-using industries[8] at
various levels of IT intensity. In that figure, all industries
in the economy are grouped into three segments. The
darkest curve represents those that use IT the most heavily,
the next darkest line those that have moderate IT use, and
the lightest line those with little IT use. The vertical axis
shows the profit disparity between the most profitable
companies in the segment and the least profitable as measured by the interquartile range (the 75th percentile minus
the 25th percentile) of the average profit margin. Until the
early 1980s, the size of differences in profit margins did
not vary much with IT intensity—that is, leading firms
were only a few percentage points better in profit margin
than lagging firms in those industries. However, since the
mid 1990s the interquartile range of profits for the heavi-
est users of IT has exploded. The difference between being
a winner and being a lagging firm in IT-intensive industries is very large and growing. Using technology effectively matters more now than ever before.

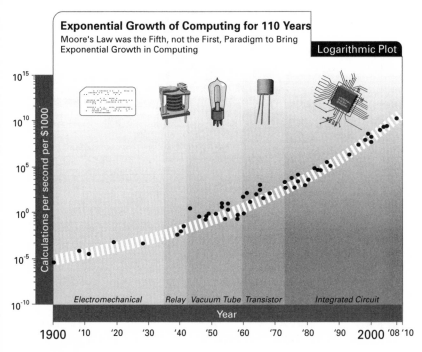

Figure 1.6
"Exponential growth of computing for 110 years." Source: KurzweilAI
.net. Used with permission.

In light of the continued innovation in IT and the disparity of profits in IT-intensive industries, this is a very important time to study technology's strategic value to businesses.

In this book, we provide a guide for policy makers and economists who want to understand how information technology is transforming the economy and where it will

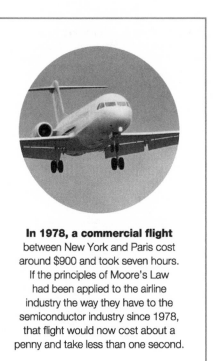

In 1978, a commercial flight
between New York and Paris cost
around $900 and took seven hours.
If the principles of Moore's Law
had been applied to the airline
industry the way they have to the
semiconductor industry since 1978,
that flight would now cost about a
penny and take less than one second.

Figure 1.7
Moore's Law in perspective. Copyright 2005 Intel Corporation.

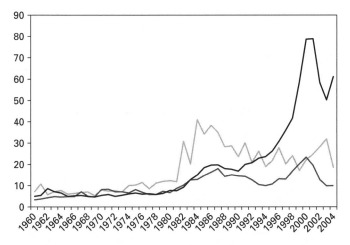

Figure 1.8
Profitability in IT-intensive industries (profit disparity between most profitable and least profitable companies in segment, as measured by interquartile range, 1960–2004). Source: Brynjolfsson, McAfee, Sorell, and Zhu 2009.

create value in the coming decade. We begin by discussing official measures of the size of the information economy and analyzing their limitations. We continue with the literature on IT, productivity, and economic growth. Next, we review the literature on business processes that enhance productivity. We look at attempts to quantify the value of these processes in the form of intangible organizational capital. We then examine the innovation literature in relation to technology, as well as other metrics of measuring the effect of technology the economy, such as consumer surplus. We conclude with a peek at emerging research.

Further Reading

Nicholas G. Carr, "IT Doesn't Matter," *Harvard Business Review* 81 (2003), no. 5: 41–49. This provocative article questions the strategic value of IT. The author sees IT near the end of its buildout and asserts that the biggest risk to IT is overspending.

Ray Kurzweil, *The Singularity Is Near: When Humans Transcend Biology* (Viking Penguin, 2005). This book predicts remarkable possibilities due to the accelerating nature of technological progress in the coming decades.

Andrew McAfee and Erik Brynjolfsson, "Investing in the IT That Makes a Competitive Difference," *Harvard Business Review* 86 (2008), no. 7/8: 98–107. The authors find that the gap between leaders and laggards has grown significantly since 1995, especially in IT-intensive industries.

2   Measuring the Information Economy

The United States is now predominantly a service-based economy. For every dollar of goods produced by the economy in 2008, about $3.61 of services was generated.[1] But this transformation of the economy did not happen suddenly. The economy has steadily moved away from producing goods and toward producing services for at least the last half-century.[2] Table 2.1 demonstrates that even in 1950 a greater share of gross domestic product was accounted for by services than by goods. For every dollar of goods produced in 1950, there was $1.19 of value produced in the service sector.

Interestingly, in 2008, what the Bureau of Economic Analysis calls "ICT-producing industries"[3] accounted for less than 4 percent of economic output—a figure that includes the production of hardware and software and also includes IT services.[4] However, the effect of technology on the economy goes far beyond its production. Indeed, the innovative use of technology by individuals,

Table 2.1
Percentage contribution to gross domestic product. Source: Bureau of Economic Analysis, Gross-Domestic-Product-by-Industry Accounts, Value Added by Industry as a Percentage of Gross Domestic Product. "ICT-producing industries" consists of computer and electronic products, publishing industries (including software), information and data processing services, and computer systems design and related services. For ICT-producing industries, the BEA has aggregate statistics going back to 1987 (when ICT consisted of 3.3 percent of the economy). Totals may not add exactly to 100 because of rounding.

	1950	1960	1970	1980	1990	2000	2008
Private sector	89.2	86.8	84.8	86.2	86.1	87.7	87.1
Goods	40.8	35.5	31.6	30.1	23.7	21.2	18.9
Services	48.5	51.4	53.2	56.1	62.4	66.5	68.2
Government	10.8	13.2	15.2	13.8	13.9	12.3	12.9
ICT-producing industries	—	—	—	—	3.4	4.7	3.8

firms, and industries makes far more of a difference to the economy.

Table 2.2 disaggregates GDP by industry groupings, the sum of the groupings' shares being 100. Manufacturing, which was more than 25 percent of the economy in 1950, is now less than half that percentage. Agriculture has shrunk the most dramatically; it is less than 20 percent as large a share of the economy as it was in 1950. The largest sector of the economy today, Finance, Insurance, and Real Estate, has nearly doubled its share since 1950. Some sectors have seen even more dramatic growth. The Education, Health Care, and Social Assistance sector has quadrupled, and

Table 2.2
Composition of gross domestic product by industry grouping (percentages). Source: Bureau of Economic Analysis, Gross-Domestic-Product-by-Industry Accounts, Value Added by Industry as a Percentage of Gross Domestic Product. Information comprises publishing (newspapers, books, periodicals), software publishing, broadcasting, telecommunications producers and distributors, motion picture and sound recording industries, and information and data processing services. Because of rounding, totals may not add up to 100.

	1950	1960	1970	1980	1990	2000	2008
Private sector	89.2	86.8	84.8	86.2	86.1	87.7	87.1
Finance, insurance, real estate, rental, leasing	11.4	14.1	14.6	15.9	18.0	19.7	20.0
Professional and business services	3.9	4.7	5.4	6.7	9.8	11.6	12.7
Wholesale and retail trade	15.1	14.5	14.5	14.0	12.9	12.7	11.9
Manufacturing	27.0	25.3	22.7	20.0	16.3	14.5	11.5
Mining, utilities, construction	8.6	8.5	8.2	10.2	8.3	7.5	8.5
Education, health care, social assistance	2.0	2.7	3.9	5.0	6.7	6.9	8.1
Information	2.7	3.0	3.4	3.5	3.9	4.7	4.4
Arts, entertainment, recreation, accommodation, food services	3.0	2.8	2.8	3.0	3.4	3.6	3.8
Transportation and warehousing	5.9	4.5	3.9	3.7	2.9	3.1	2.9
Other services	2.8	2.9	2.6	2.2	2.5	2.3	2.3
Agriculture, forestry, fishing, hunting	6.8	3.8	2.6	2.2	1.7	1.0	1.1
Government	10.8	13.2	15.2	13.8	13.9	12.3	12.9

Table 2.3
Information-processing equipment investment (nonresidential private-sector fixed investment in equipment and software) as a percentage of nonresidential private-sector fixed investment in equipment. Source: Bureau of Economic Analysis, National Income and Products Account, Table 5.3.5, "Private Fixed Investment by Type." Other information-processing equipment includes communication equipment; non-medical instruments; medical equipment and instruments; photocopy and related equipment; and office and accounting equipment. Totals may not add exactly to 100 because of rounding.

	1960	1970	1980	1990	2000	2008
Information-processing equipment	16.4	24.2	30.4	42.2	50.9	53.6
Computers and peripherals	0.7	3.9	5.5	9.2	11.0	9.0
Software	0.3	3.3	4.3	11.3	19.2	24.1
Other	15.4	16.9	20.5	21.7	20.7	20.6
Non-information-processing equipment	83.9	75.8	69.6	57.8	49.1	46.4

Professional and Business Services has tripled as a share of the economy. As a share of GDP, the Information sector is more than 4 percent of the economy, more than 60 percent larger than it was in 1950 relative to other industries.

Information-processing equipment (hardware, software, communications equipment, and other equipment such as photocopiers) accounts for half of all business investment in equipment. (See table 2.3.)

Figure 2.1 clarifies how the Bureau of Economic Analysis aggregates industries as either "Information" industries or "ICT-producing" industries.

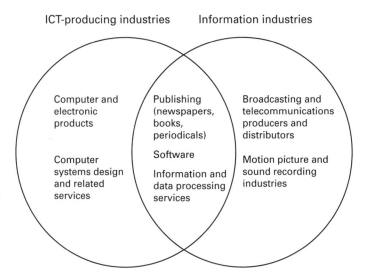

ICT-producing industries   Information industries

Computer and
electronic
products

Computer
systems design
and related
services

Publishing
(newspapers,
books,
periodicals)

Software

Information and
data processing
services

Broadcasting and
telecommunications
producers and
distributors

Motion picture and
sound recording
industries

Figure 2.1
Comparison of Bureau of Economic Analysis aggregates.

Although the statistics in tables 2.1–2.3 cover the economy as a whole, they do not reflect the outsized influence that ICT and information industries have on innovation. We explore this relationship by disaggregating venture-capital (VC) investments into various industries and totaling the shares to 100.

Annual VC investment grew by more than a factor of 10 between 1995 and 2000. Today, less than one-third as much is invested per year as at the peak of the bubble. Despite the enormous change in total VC investment, ICT and information and entertainment industries have accounted for 50–75 percent of all venture-capital

Table 2.4
Venture capital investment, 1997–2007, by industry. Sources: PricewaterhouseCoopers; National Venture Capital Association, *MoneyTree Report*. Information and Entertainment Industries comprises IT services, media and entertainment, software, and telecommunications. ICT-producing industries comprises computers and peripherals, electronics, networking and equipment, and semiconductors.

	1997	1998	1999	2000	2001	2002	2003	2004	2005	2006	2007
Information and entertainment industries	44.7	49.2	54.9	57.6	50.7	43.1	40.6	40.2	40.7	39.8	36.3
ICT-producing industries	15.1	12.8	12.9	17.0	22.6	22.9	20.9	20.7	18.9	16.6	14.9
Biotechnology	9.5	7.5	3.9	4.0	8.5	14.8	18.5	19.0	16.7	17.5	16.9
Medical devices	6.9	5.6	2.9	2.4	5.1	8.4	8.5	8.6	9.7	10.7	13.3
Industrial and energy industries	4.9	6.9	3.1	2.4	2.8	3.4	3.9	3.5	3.7	7.2	10.4
Financial services	2.5	3.9	4.1	4.0	3.6	1.6	2.1	2.3	4.0	1.8	1.8
Business products and services	3.1	3.3	5.2	4.8	2.7	2.3	3.1	1.8	1.7	2.2	2.5
Healthcare	6.0	4.4	2.7	1.3	1.2	1.6	1.2	1.6	1.7	1.5	0.9
Consumer products and services	5.0	3.1	4.8	3.3	1.7	1.1	0.9	1.4	1.6	1.9	1.6
Retailing	2.1	3.0	5.3	3.0	0.8	0.7	0.4	0.8	1.0	0.8	1.3
Other	0.2	0.2	0.1	0.0	0.2	0.1	0.0	0.0	0.2	0.0	0.0
Total venture capital invested (billions of dollars)	14.9	21.1	54.0	104.9	40.6	22.0	19.8	22.5	23.1	26.7	30.8

investments in the United States in every year since 1995.

Therefore, less than 10 percent of the economy drives well over half of the venture investment taking place in the United States today. Other than its outsized effect on innovation, technology is having another large influence on everyday life not counted in the tables above—in transactions that take place outside traditional markets.

GDP Largely Excludes Non-Market Transactions

GDP is primarily a measure of *market* transactions for new goods and services. Economic activity outside the market[6] and market transactions in used goods and services[7] will generally not be included in the National Income and Product Accounts (the official name of the GDP statistics). For example, a 20-minute visit to www.nytimes.com to read the latest news will not affect GDP. Walking to the newsstand and picking up the print edition of the *New York Times*, however, will add $1.50 to GDP whether you read the paper or not. Likewise, planning one's vacation by searching the Web and then going to Lonely Planet's Thorn Tree Forums will not have any direct effect on GDP, but paying for a guidebook at the local bookstore will add to GDP.

Or take Google and Yahoo, which between them currently share approximately 80 percent of the search-engine market.[8] They offer dozens of services, most of which are completely free to consumers. Keyword searches, by far their most popular tool, have made millions of people better off. Because these searches are free, their value to consumers does not show up in the National Accounts. The primary way that these search engines generate revenue is through selling targeted keyword advertisements that appear on the side of the page when a user performs a search. The revenue-generating segment of the market—advertising sales—is a part of the *measurable* output of Google or Yahoo because it involves market transactions. But what about the value of the searches themselves?

A significant amount of non-market activity in the economy is due to information technology. One reason for this is the principle of *information complements*—two information goods that have highly complementary demands, such as Adobe's Reader and Acrobat (Parker and Van Alstyne 2005). Adobe implemented a very successful strategy in encouraging the widespread adoption of the PDF format. Because Adobe gave Reader away to one side of the market, the other side of the market for PDF-writing software (such as Acrobat) has grown tremendously. Because Adobe does not sell Reader, GDP will not measure the aggregate value of Reader. GDP only includes the purchases of Acrobat and other PDF writers. Consider also the aggregate value of all the free software available online. In addition to Adobe's Reader, the benefits to consumers from the free software in CNET's "Download Hall of Fame" (such as QuickTime, ICQ, and Winamp) are not reflected in the National Accounts either.[9]

In addition to the workplace, technology has also an important effect outside the office. Take Internet use, for example. The current GDP methods assume that the value of Internet access is strictly the amount that people pay their Internet Service Providers (ISPs). So when tens of millions of people watch videos on YouTube for free, the GDP sees nothing. When tens of millions of people watch videos on YouTube for free, the GDP sees nothing. Clearly, monthly ISP fees underestimate the total contribution of the Internet to consumers. Goolsbee and Klenow (2006) point out that only 0.2 percent of American consumption spending is on Internet access but Americans spend more than 10 percent of their leisure time online. Goolsbee and Klenow used a non-traditional method in an attempt to derive total consumer surplus from Internet access. First, they show that if they use data on how much money people spend (the traditional method of valuing consumer welfare) the median consumer receives about $100 in benefits from ISPs by using the Internet. If Goolsbee and Klenow use the metric of time spent online instead, they estimate that the median consumer is $3,000 better off!

The US government, recognizing that time spent may be a better way than dollars spent to measure certain economic benefits to consumers, recently began publishing an American Time Use Survey. First published in 2004, the annual survey studies about 12,000 individuals over the age of 15. According to the 2007 survey, Americans spent only 3.8 hours per day in income-generating work-related activities (when averaged among all individuals over the age of 15). If this number seems low, that is because it includes people who don't work for pay (e.g., students, retirees, and the unemployed) and days on which most people don't work (e.g., Saturdays, Sundays, and holidays). That leaves a lot of time that is not spent working for pay. The question is how to best measure the value of the time that Americans are not working. Nordhaus (2006) notes that a standard way to value leisure is to measure after-tax income but points out some of the problems inherent in this kind of estimate. People typically cannot sell an extra hour of their time at their going wage rate at will unless they are self-employed. Even then, the *marginal* wage of a self-employed person may be different from his or her *average* wage. In addition, the value of time to people can vary highly, depending on the time of day—something that standard calculations do not take into account.

The US government does attempt to calculate the value of transactions that occur outside of officially tracked markets in the National Accounts. About 15 percent of GDP is imputed or calculated from non-market data.[10] The largest segment of this imputed value is the rental value of owner-occupied housing.[11] However, Abraham and Mackie (2006, p. 168) also identify significant amounts of non-market activity that are not measured in GDP. One example is in health care. Whereas the cost of health care is measured in GDP, the value of improvements to health or quality of life are not captured directly in GDP. Research suggests that this omission alone may be worth nearly as much as the increased value of all other goods and services since 1950 (Nordhaus 2005).

How Government Measures Industry

In order to understand how the US government currently defines industries and price indices, it is useful to briefly trace the history of how the government has measured GDP and prices. Until the 1930s, government statistics were quite difficult to compare across government agencies, because each agency had its own definition of industries (Pearce 1957). The Standard Industrial Classification (SIC) was developed in the 1930s in an effort to standardize industry definitions. When the SIC was adopted, it consisted of four-digit codes for each industry, with a primary focus on the manufacturing sector. (See box 2.1.)

It became clear in the 1990s that the SIC system was not finely detailed enough to capture the changes that were taking place in the economy. This was especially true in the Information sector, which had subcomponents

Box 2.1
A Brief History of Industrial Classification

• 1930s: First developed
• 1941: First printed edition of Manufacturing Industries
• 1942: First printed edition of Non-Manufacturing Industries
• 1945: Manufacturing Industries revised
• 1949: Non-Manufacturing Industries revised
• 1957: Manufacturing Industries and Non-Manufacturing Industries first combined into one book
• 1972: Major revision of codes
• 1987: Major revision of codes
• 1997: Canadian and American statistical agencies switch to North American Industry Classification System (NAICS) (Mexican agencies switch in 1998)
• 2002: NAICS codes revised
• 2007: NAICS codes revised

---

scattered across various other industries. The United States and Canada switched to the North American Classification System (NAICS) in 1997, and Mexico switched in 1998. The number of broad sectors also increased from 10 to 20. For example, "Services" in SIC was divided into seven broad kinds of sectors, including the Information Sector. Table 2.5 illustrates the difference between NAICS and SIC.

One example of the importance of industry reclassification is the Information sector. According to the old SIC

Table 2.5
Comparison of North American Industry Classification System and Standard Industry Classification. Source: NAICS. Available at www.naics.com.

Broad two-digit NAICS code	NAICS sector	SIC division
11	Agriculture, Forestry, Fishing, and Hunting	Agriculture, Forestry, and Fishing
21	Mining	Mining
23	Construction	Construction
31–33	Manufacturing	Manufacturing
22	Utilities	Transportation, Communications, and Public Utilities
48–49	Transportation and Warehousing	
42	Wholesale Trade	Wholesale Trade
44–45	Retail Trade	Retail Trade
72	Accommodation and Food Services	
52	Finance and Insurance	Finance, Insurance, and Real Estate
53	Real Estate and Rental and Leasing	
51	Information	Services
54	Professional, Scientific, and Technical Services	
56	Administrative and Support; Waste Management and Remediation Services	

Table 2.5
(continued)

Broad two-digit NAICS code	NAICS sector	SIC division
61	Educational Services	
62	Health Care and Social Assistance	
71	Arts, Entertainment and Recreation	
81	Other Services (except Public Administration)	
92	Public Administration	Public Administration
55	Management of Companies and Enterprises	(Parts of all divisions)

system last updated in 1987, Google would fall under 737, Computer Programming, Data Processing, and Other Computer Related Services. Under the new NAICS system, Google is classified in industry 519130, Internet Publishing and Web Search Portals. (See table 2.6.)

How Government Measures the Consumer Price Index

When people buy goods and services, they consider more than the price. They also look at quality, convenience, timeliness, and other attributes. However, these other attributes are usually not priced explicitly, so measuring how these factors affect prices has been difficult. Although

Table 2.6
Detailed classification of the information sector.

2007 NAICS code	
51	Information
511	Publishing industries (except Internet)
5111	Newspaper, Periodical, Book, and Directory Publishers
511110	Newspaper publishers
511120	Periodical publishers
511130	Book publishers
511140	Directory and mailing list publishers
51119	Other publishers
511191	Greeting card publishers
511199	All other publishers
5112	Software publishers
511210	Software publishers
512	Motion picture and sound recording industries
5121	Motion picture and video industries
512110	Motion picture and video production
512120	Motion picture and video distribution
51213	Motion picture and video exhibition
512131	Motion picture theaters (except drive-ins)
512132	Drive-in motion picture theaters
51219	Postproduction services and other motion picture and video industries
512191	Teleproduction and other postproduction services
512199	Other motion picture and video industries
5122	Sound recording industries
512210	Record production
512220	Integrated record production/ distribution

Table 2.6
(continued)

2007 NAICS code	
512230	Music publishers
512240	Sound recording studios
512290	Other sound recording industries
515	Broadcasting (except Internet)
5151	Radio and television broadcasting
515111	Radio networks
515112	Radio stations
515120	Television broadcasting
5152	Cable and other subscription programming
515210	Cable and other subscription programming
517	Telecommunications
517110	Wired telecommunications carriers
517210	Wireless telecommunications carriers (except satellite)
517410	Satellite telecommunications
51791	Other telecommunications
517911	Telecommunications resellers
517919	All other telecommunications
518	Data processing, hosting, and related services
518210	Data processing, hosting, and related services
519	Other information services
519110	News syndicates
519120	Libraries and archives
519130	Internet publishing and broadcasting and Web search portals
519190	All other information services

the government began publishing the Consumer Price Index in 1919,[12] it did not attempt to reflect changes in product quality adjustments in the CPI until World War II (Nordhaus 1997, p. 56).

Two major congressional commissions, one in 1961 and one in 1996, came to a similar conclusion—that the CPI was overstating the true rate of inflation because the Bureau of Labor Statistics did not take into account quality adjustments in goods (such as 1913 cars compared to 2008 cars). In 1961, the Stigler Commission concluded that the CPI did not take into account substitution bias—the fact that consumers substitute away from higher-priced goods to lower-priced substitutes as they become available, such as substituting away from an expensive tube-based radio to a cheaper transistor radio. The Stigler Commission recommended using a more representative, random sample of prices for the CPI, and also argued for a constant utility index—i.e., that the CPI should measure how much it would cost to maintain a set amount of utility, rather than how much it would cost to purchase a fixed basket of goods.

In 1996, the Boskin Commission estimated that, because of numerous biases (associated with the delay of introducing new goods, quality changes, consumers switching from higher-priced goods to lower-priced goods, and consumers switching from higher-priced stores to low-cost outlets), the CPI overestimated inflation by about 1.1 percentage points per year. Because spending on federal

programs such as Social Security is indexed to rise auto-
matically with the CPI, the Boskin Commission estimated
that a trillion dollars would be added to the national
debt by 2008 if the recommended changes were not
made. Although the Bureau of Labor Statistics implemented some of the changes recommended by the
Boskin Commission, Gordon (2006) estimates that the
remaining bias in the CPI is still as much as 0.8 percentage
points per year. Insofar as inflation (measured as the
December-to-December change in the CPI) averaged 2.5
percent per year from 1999 to 2008, this bias is quite
significant.

The prices of most goods increase every year, but computers are an exception: huge price declines and quality
improvements are pervasive year after year. On March 2,
1987, Apple introduced its first personal computer that
could display color graphics. That was the Macintosh II,
which started at $3,898 and included one floppy-disk
drive but no monitor. With add-ons such as a color
monitor, an 80-MB hard drive, and IBM compatibility, a
Macintosh II could cost as much as $10,000. Today one can
buy a computer with 100 times the performance for a frac-
tion of that price. Nordhaus (2007) estimates that computing has improved 18–20 percent per year—that is, by a
factor of 2 trillion to 76 trillion, depending on the measure
used—over the mechanical adding machines of 1850. In
late 1985, the Bureau of Economic Analysis began measuring quality-adjusted prices for computers, and in 1996 it
introduced techniques to reduce the substitution bias for

computers in the CPI (Stiroh 2002, p. 48). From 1998 to 2003, the Bureau of Labor Statistics measured the value of quality improvements in computing by using hedonic regressions to determine the value of various components of a computer and its peripherals, such as memory or a printer (Bureau of Labor Statistics 2008). A hedonic regression subdivides a computer into its various subcomponents to estimate the contribution of each subcomponent to the computer's value. If the price of the computer stays constant from one year to the next, but various subcomponents of the computer such as speed and memory improve, a hedonic regression estimates the resulting change in value. Since 2003, the Bureau of Labor Statistics has instead measured the direct value of components using prices found on the Internet to make the necessary changes to the quality-adjusted prices of computers. For example, desktop computers are divided into 250–300 subcomponents, of which the prices are updated monthly. Table 2.7 puts these price and quality changes into perspective. In the first column is what it would have cost in that year to purchase a market basket of goods and services equivalent to one that could be had for $4,000 in 1987. It consistently goes up. After 20 years, it cost 83 percent more to buy the same market basket (based on, for instance, the prices of fuel, food, transportation, doctor's visits, and thousands of other goods) than in 1987. However, the prices of computers not only went in the opposite direction; they went way, way down. In 2007, to purchase $4,000 worth of 1987 computing power would have cost only $40!

Table 2.7
A 20-year comparison of the costs of computers and purchasing power. Source: Authors' calculations, based on unpublished Bureau of Labor Statistics data for the PC deflator. CPI is the annual average from the Bureau of Labor Statistics.

	What it would cost to maintain $4,000 worth of 1987's purchasing power	What it would cost to purchase the quality of a $4,000 1987 computer
1987	$4,000.00	$4,000.00
1992	$4,940.14	$1,828.20
1997	$5,651.41	$465.88
2002	$6,334.51	$92.03
2007	$7,300.77	$38.24

The Changing Composition of the Dow Jones Industrial Average

The Dow Jones Industrial Average provides a useful comparison to government measures of the economy. First published in 1896 as an index of 12 large industrial companies, "The Dow" has become one of the best-known private-sector measures of the economy. Only one of twelve original companies is still in the Dow today: General Electric.[13] In 1928, the average grew to its current size of 30 companies. On rare occasions, the managing editor of the *Wall Street Journal* changes the companies in the average to reflect the composition of the US economy. (Since 1995, there have been six replacements in the Dow.) Each company added to the Dow is selected as a representative of a sector of the economy.[14]

Table 2.8 shows a side-by-side comparison of the components of the Dow at four points in time, to illustrate the dynamic turnover among this set of leading companies since 1950. Only seven companies or their descendents remain out of the 30 companies on the 1950 list. Some of the changes represent simple competition—for example, Wal-Mart out-retailed Sears, and Caterpillar overtook International Harvester. In other cases, entire industries disappeared—all three steel companies from 1950 fell from the list. Some businesses in the Dow have undergone shifts in their core business—IBM was a maker of office equipment, then a computer manufacturer, and now is primarily providing IT services. And new companies representing entirely new industries (e.g., Intel and Microsoft) have appeared. The US economy is very dynamic.

Despite the considerable changes in the makeup of the Dow, the majority of the companies included in it today are manufacturing firms. About 40 percent of the Dow companies primarily make non-physical products (e.g. Microsoft) or are primarily engaged in services (e.g. Walt Disney). What is most interesting about the Dow's tilt toward manufacturing is that producers of goods account for only 20 percent of the overall US economy. (See table 2.1.)

Table 2.8
Companies included in the Dow Jones Industrial Average. Source: Dow Jones Company. Available at http://www.djindexes.com.

1950	1970	1990	2009
Allied Chemical	Allied Chemical	Allied-Signal	3M
American Can	Aluminum Company of America	Aluminum Company of America	Alcoa
American Smelting	American Can	American Express	American Express
American Telephone and Telegraph	American Telephone and Telegraph	American Telephone and Telegraph	AT&T
American Tobacco B	American Tobacco B	Bethlehem Steel	Bank of America
Bethlehem Steel	Anaconda Copper	Boeing	Boeing
Chrysler	Bethlehem Steel	Chevron	Caterpillar
Corn Products Refining	Chrysler	Coca-Cola	Chevron
DuPont	DuPont	DuPont	Cisco Systems
Eastman Kodak	Eastman Kodak	Eastman Kodak	Coca-Cola
General Electric	General Electric	Exxon	DuPont
General Foods	General Foods	General Electric	ExxonMobil
General Motors	General Motors	General Motors	General Electric
Goodyear			Hewlett-Packard

International Harvester	Goodyear	Goodyear	Home Depot
International Nickel	International Harvester	International Business Machines	Intel
Johns-Manville	International Nickel	International Paper	International Business Machines
Loew's	International Paper	McDonald's	Johnson & Johnson
National Distillers	Johns-Manville	Merck	JPMorgan Chase
National Steel	Owens-Illinois Glass	Minnesota Mining & Mfg.	Kraft Foods
Procter & Gamble	Procter & Gamble	Navistar International	McDonald's
Sears, Roebuck	Sears, Roebuck	Philip Morris	Merck
Standard Oil of California	Standard Oil of California	Primerica	Microsoft
Standard Oil (NJ)	Standard Oil (NJ)	Procter & Gamble	Pfizer
Texas Company	Swift	Sears, Roebuck	Procter & Gamble
Union Carbide	Texaco	Texaco	Travelers
United Aircraft	Union Carbide	Union Carbide	United Technologies
U.S. Steel	United Aircraft	United Technologies	Verizon
Westinghouse Electric	U.S. Steel	USX	Wal-Mart Stores
Woolworth	Westinghouse Electric	Westinghouse Electric	Walt Disney
	Woolworth	Woolworth	

Summary

Which would you prefer to have: $40,000 to spend on goods and services available in 2008 at 2008 prices, or $400,000 to spend at 1913 prices but only on goods and services that were available in 1913 (e.g., no big-screen TVs or penicillin)? This hypothetical comparison is the essence of estimating more than 90 years of changes in the standard of living. In addition to the new goods available today, the improved quality and timeliness of many existing goods reflect the contributions of information technology. These aspects are not as easily quantifiable as prices. As a result, the biggest shortcoming of how the government has historically measured prices is that it has not measured these quality changes and product introductions. Even one of the best-known private-sector indices of the economy, the Dow Jones Industrial Average, is disproportionally driven by companies in the manufacturing industry, despite the predominance of service industries in the economy.

Further Reading

Robert J. Gordon, "The Boskin Commission Report: A Retrospective One Decade Later," *International Productivity Monitor* 1 (2006), no. 12: 7–22. One of the five members of the Boskin Commission gives an accessible summary of its final report, the aftermath, and current measurement issues in the CPI.

William Nordhaus, "Do Real Output and Real Wage Measures Capture Reality? The History of Light Suggests Not," in *The Economics of New Goods*, ed. T. Bresnahan and R. Gordon (University of Chicago Press, 1997). A fascinating study of the real cost of lighting through the ages, with implications for how we mismeasure the cost of living.

Geoffrey Parker and Marshall Van Alstyne, "Two-Sided Network Effects: A Theory of Information Product Design," *Management Science* 51 (2005), no. 10: 1494–1504. A theoretical paper demonstrating how it can be profitable to give away free goods on one side of an information-goods market to boost sales on the other side of the market.

Marshall Reinsdorf and Jack Triplett, "A Review of Reviews: Ninety Years of Professional Thinking About the Consumer Price Index," in *Price Index Concepts and Measurement*, ed. E. Diewert et al. (University of Chicago Press, forthcoming). A comprehensive history of reviews of the CPI.

3   IT's Contributions to Productivity and Economic Growth

For decades, companies bought computers on the promise that the "computer age" would revolutionize business. As early as 1970, hardware, software, and other technical equipment accounted for about one-fourth of all business investment in equipment. But then researchers looked at the effect of these investments. A number of studies in the 1980s and the 1990s failed to find any evidence for the contribution of IT to productivity (Roach 1987; Loveman 1994; Berndt and Morrison 1995). In the 1980s and the early 1990s, the "productivity paradox" was debated. (For a summary and a discussion, see Brynjolfsson 1993 and Brynjolfsson and Yang 1996.) Why would firms invest so heavily in technology for decades if there wasn't a measurable effect in productivity? In 1987 the economist Robert Solow described this puzzle as follows: "You can see the computer age everywhere but in the productivity statistics."

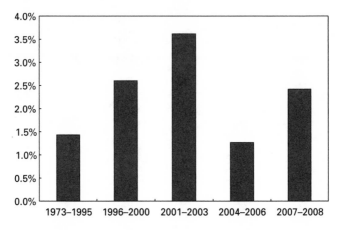

Figure 3.1
U.S. labor productivity growth (annual increase in labor productivity
in non-farm business sector) since 1973. Source: Bureau of Labor
Statistics. Cumulative annual growth rate of output per hour of the
non-farm business sector at an annualized rate. Data are for fourth
quarter before period to fourth quarter of end of period; for example,
the first bar represents the fourth quarter of 1972 through the fourth
quarter of 1995.

It is not difficult to understand the skepticism about
computers' potential to transform productivity. Lackluster
US labor productivity growth, averaging just 1.4 percent
per year from 1973 to 1995 (figure 3.1), was of great
concern to economists and policy makers. Why? Because
of the rule of 70. If you want to find out how long it takes
for something to double, you use the rule of 70. At 1
percent growth per year, it would take about 70 years for
something to double. At 2 percent, though, it would take
only $70/2 = 35$ years, and so forth.[1] At 2.7 percent—the

average growth rate of productivity from 1948 to 1972—
it took less than 26 years to double the standard of living.
At 1.4 percent, it would take 50 years.

In 1996, however, productivity growth accelerated,
averaging about 2.6 percent per year until 2000. There is
widespread agreement about the cause of this surge
in productivity growth: information technology. Dale
Jorgenson noted in his 2001 presidential address to the
American Economic Association that declines in the price
of IT "enhanced the role of IT investment as a source of
American economic growth" and that "computers have
now left an indelible imprint on the productivity statistics." Oliner and Sichel (2002, p. 15) wrote that "both the
use of information technology and efficiency gains associated with the *production* of information technology were
central factors in that [productivity] resurgence." As
Gordon (2004, p. 118) noted, the first major growth-
accounting papers to detail the productivity resurgence
(Jorgenson and Stiroh 2000; Oliner and Sichel 2000) attributed this productivity uptick to increased IT investment.
Robert Solow has since remarked to us that he no longer
has any doubts about the importance of IT in the increase
in productivity.

Organizational Investments Create a Second Surge

Not only did productivity increase from 1995 to 2000; it
increased even further in 2001–2003, to about 3.6 percent

per year. The reasons for the second surge in productivity initially caused some debate in the economics literature (Council of Economic Advisers 2004, 2006; Gordon 2004). Jorgenson, Ho, and Stiroh (2008, p. 4) argue that this second surge is fundamentally different from the one from 1995 to 2000, which was led by IT investment and productivity improvements in IT producers. From 2000 on, IT does not take the direct credit it did before. Rather, economy-wide productivity growth is driven by innovations in both products and processes in the industries that are the most intensive users of IT (rather than the IT producers). Jorgenson et al. further note that "the remainder likely reflects some combination of increased competitive pressures on firms, cyclical factors, and efficiency gains outside of the production of information technology, but some uncertainty about the underlying forces remains" (ibid., p. 4).

Our belief is that the more recent surge is the result of IT, but in the form of a "reap and harvest" story. Specifically, we are now reaping the fruits of the organizational investments that were planted in the late 1990s, made alongside the investments in hardware (Yang and Brynjolfsson 2001). The full effects on productivity from the reorganization of business processes can take several years to develop (Brynjolfsson and Hitt 2003), as intangible assets are created. If businesses harvest the benefits of earlier intangible investments while skimping on investments for the future, measured productivity growth will be temporarily boosted. Indeed, the Council of Economic Advisers (2007) agrees with this view.

Explaining the Productivity Growth of 2004–2008

This second surge in productivity was short-lived, because the same investments in business processes which were made alongside the large-scale technology investments at the end of the 1990s were not made in the early 2000s. Productivity picked up again in 2007 and 2008, we believe, because investments in IT and related process changes were made in 2003–04. Since these investments take years to pay off, investments in 2003–04 would potentially be reflected in the 2007–08 statistics. However, it is too early to tell a definitive story about productivity growth during this period.

Industry-Level Studies Reveal the Sources of Growth

The sources-of-growth model (pioneered by Robert Solow) represents economic growth as a combination of two parts: hours worked and productivity growth. Average labor productivity is defined as output per hour. In the sources-of-growth model, average labor productivity is the sum of three major sources: capital deepening, labor quality, and multi-factor productivity (often referred to as total factor productivity).

Capital deepening means using more capital per worker. All else being equal, if you give workers better and faster tools to do the job, they should be more productive. There is a nice example about the dramatic improvements in capital for agriculture over the last 200 years in the Council of Economic Advisers' 2007 report (pp. 47–48). In 1830, it took 250–300 hours for a farmer to produce 100 bushels of wheat. In 1890, with horse-drawn machines, it took only 40–50 hours to produce the same amount. By 1975, with large tractors and combines, a farmer could produce 100 bushels of wheat in only 3–4 hours.

Labor quality reflects education and skills. It represents the contribution of improvements in human capital to productivity.

Multi-factor productivity (MFP) encompasses the other factors that are not classified as capital deepening or labor quality. It is modeled as the residual or leftover part of productivity that can't be directly inferred from capital and labor. The Council of Economic Advisers (2007, pp. 48–49) notes that the following contribute to MFP growth: product improvements or process improvements such as reorganizing the factory floor, and entrepreneurship, which involves inventing new methods of doing business.

In table 3.1 we highlight recent calculations by Jorgenson, Ho, and Stiroh (2008) that use the sources-of-growth model to analyze productivity growth in the US economy since 1959. Capital deepening is divided into

Table 3.1
Sources of growth in U.S. private economy. Source: Jorgenson, Ho, and Stiroh 2008, p.13. All growth rates are in percent per year. IT includes computer hardware, software, and communications equipment. Share attributed to IT: average contribution of IT capital deepening plus the average contribution of IT multi-factor productivity divided by average labor productivity for each period.

	1959–2006	1959–1973	1973–1995	1995–2000	2000–2006
Private output growth (average annual)	3.58	4.18	3.08	4.77	3.01
Hours worked	1.44	1.36	1.59	2.07	0.51
Average labor productivity	2.14	2.82	1.49	2.70	2.50
Contribution of capital deepening	1.14	1.40	0.85	1.51	1.26
IT	0.43	0.21	0.40	1.01	0.58
Non-IT	0.70	1.19	0.45	0.49	0.69
Contribution of labor quality	0.26	0.28	0.25	0.19	0.31
Multi-factor productivity	0.75	1.14	0.39	1.00	0.92
IT	0.25	0.09	0.25	0.58	0.38
Non-IT	0.49	1.05	0.14	0.42	0.54
Share attributed to IT	0.32	0.11	0.43	0.59	0.38

investment in computer hardware, software, and communications equipment and investment in non-IT equipment and structures. Multi-factor productivity is divided into improvements in the IT-producing industries and improvements in the IT-using (or non-IT-producing) industries. Note that the IT-related contribution from capital deepening went from 0.40 percent per year in the period 1973–1995 to 1.01 percent per year in the period 1995–2000, and that MFP due to IT producers went from 0.25 to 0.58 percent per year. Jorgenson, Ho, and Stiroh (p. 13) note that these two increases account for almost 80 percent of the productivity increase from 1973–1995 to 1995–2000. This can be found by comparing the columns. Productivity grew from 1.49 to 2.70 percent per year, a difference of 1.21 percent per year. IT capital deepening grew 0.61 percentage points (1.01–0.40), and the IT producers in MFP grew 0.33 percentage points (0.58–0.25), giving these two sources 0.94 percentage points out of 1.21, which is 78 percent of the increase.

Yet we see a very different IT story in the period 2000–2006. The contribution of IT capital deepening in 2000–2006 falls to only 0.58 percentage points per year (from 1.01 percentage points per year in 1995–2000), and the contribution of IT producers to MFP falls from 0.58 percent in the 1995–2000 period to 0.38 percent in the period 2000–2006. Overall, the share of productivity growth due to direct, measurable contributions from IT falls quite a lot—from 0.59 in 1995–2000 to 0.38 in 2000–2006. Yet during this time the contribution of MFP from IT-using industries increased from 0.42 to 0.54 percentage points per year. We believe that some of this MFP growth among IT users in 2000–2006 represents the fruits of the business-process redesign and other reengineering efforts that were made alongside technology investments from 1995 to 2000.

How IT Investment Explains Some Productivity, But Not All

Although scholars agree that technology has played an important role in the productivity acceleration, there is far less agreement on the extent to which IT has contributed to this productivity revival. Stiroh (2004) examined dozens of productivity papers and took an in-depth look at 20 production function estimates. He found a large body of work supporting the hypothesis that IT is responsible for the increase in post-1995 productivity. But he also noted that methodological differences between studies created a wide variation in the estimates of the size of its effect.

Figure 3.2 illustrates the wide variety of potential returns to IT investment using more than 1,000 data points gathered from firm-level data (as shown in Brynjolfsson and Hitt 2000, p. 32). Although investment in IT is positively correlated with productivity, there are large differences between firms. Some firms reap extraordinary productivity gains from IT; others see little or no gain.

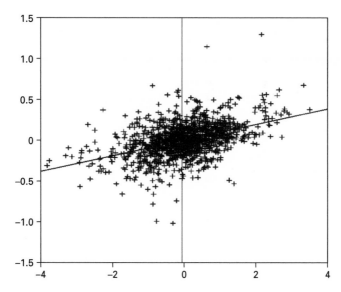

Figure 3.2
Multi-factor productivity in relation to a firm's IT assets. Adapted from
Brynjolfsson and Hitt 2000, p. 32. Horizontal axis represents number of
standard deviations of IT assets that a firm has relative to industry
average. Vertical axis represents how far each firm's multi-factor productivity is above or below industry average.

Several studies illustrate the importance of IT-related
organizational change. Brynjolfsson and Hitt (2000, p. 45),
who survey mostly firm-level studies of productivity, find
that "computers have had an impact on economic growth
that is disproportionately large compared to their share of
capital stock or investment, and that this impact is likely to
grow further in coming years." They point to the complementary investments in new business processes skills, and
to new organizational and industry structures as a "major

driver of the contribution of information technology." Dedrick, Gurbaxani, and Kraemer (2003, p. 23) survey about 50 empirical studies of information technology and productivity from 1985 to 2002 and similarly find strong evidence that complementary investments in organizational capital "have a major impact on returns to IT investments." Fernald and Ramnath (2004) also conclude that the productivity acceleration after 1995 went beyond simply the IT-producing industries. They argue that "it appears that ICT users themselves introduced a lot of innovations in the way they did business" (p. 61). For example, according to the McKinsey Global Institute's 2001 report, Wal-Mart played an important role both directly and indirectly in increasing US pro-ductivity in the service sector in the 1990s. Wal-Mart's IT-intensive business practices and its large productivity advantage over its competitors spurred a revolution in the retailing industry by encouraging other retailers to adopt some of its best practices.

Country-Level Comparison: Why the US Economy Is Different

From 1996 through 2007, the US economy was more productive than the average of the economies in either the G7, the Euro-zone, or the OECD.[2] Various studies attribute much of the difference to either the intensity of IT use by US firms or to complementary assets. Colecchia and Schreyer (2002), who performed a macro-level analysis of the returns of IT capital in nine OECD countries, find that, although all these countries experienced increases in economic growth due to IT investments, the effects were "clearly largest in the United States" (p. 432). Dewan and Kraemer (2000) provide economy-wide estimates of the contribution of IT investment to productivity in a panel of 36 countries from 1985 to 1993. They conclude that returns to IT investments in developed countries are positive, whereas returns in developing countries are not statistically significant. They suggest that the lack of complementary assets, such as basic infrastructure or human capital, may be an explanation for the divergent results. Using industry-level data, Basu et al. (2003) argue that investments in intangible organizational capital can explain why productivity accelerated so rapidly in 1995 in the United States but not in the United Kingdom. Pilat (2004), who surveyed IT and productivity studies across OECD countries, also concludes that "ICT related changes are part of a process of search and experimentation, where some firms succeed and grow and others fail and disappear. Countries with a business environment that enables this process of creative destruction may be better able to seize benefits from ICT than countries where such changes are more difficult and slow to occur." (p. 58)

Summary

The literature on productivity in the period 1995–2008 confirms that IT is playing an important role in the US

Box 3.1
Technology, Centralization, and the Boundaries of the Firm

How will technology affect the management and size of companies? Leavitt and Whisler, in their 1958 *Harvard Business Review* article "Management in the 1980s," were among the first to ask "How will technology transform firms?" (They were among the first to even use the term *information technology*.) They predicted that technology would centralize decision making in organizations. In particular, they suggested that information technology would allow information to flow to the top, where decisions would be made. Individuals on the front line would not have to make decisions, which would make their lives easier: "For some classes of jobs and people, the advent of impersonal rules may offer protection or relief from frustration. We recently heard, for example, of efforts to program a maintenance foreman's decisions by providing rules for allocating priorities in maintenance and emergency repairs. The foreman supported this fully. He was a harried and much blamed man, and programming promised relief." (p. 45) This argument reflected the prevailing beliefs in the merits of top-down management at the time—that technology would lead to increased centralization of decision making through better information flows.

This view of technology-supported centralization in the organization of the future has changed 180 degrees. One provocative vision comes from Thomas Malone. In his 2004 book *The Future of Work*, he argues that the future organization will resemble a democracy. Instead of top-down control, companies will use technology to deploy distributed decision making schemes such as voting and internal markets.

Technology will also affect the boundaries of the firm. Coase (1937) authored the classic paper about the boundaries of the firm by considering two extremes in firm size. On one hand, he asked why there are any firms at all (that is, why is the economy not made up entirely of entrepreneurs). After all, markets had a good track record of efficiently allocating most resources. On the other hand, he considered that a larger firm, because of economies of scale, might be more cost efficient than a smaller firm. Then why wasn't there just one large firm that produced everything in the world? Coase argued that the boundaries of the firm reflected tradeoffs between what could be better accomplished inside the firm by efficient scale and what was best done outside the firm by markets. Thoroughly exploring this tradeoff is well beyond the scope of this paper (see Gibbons 2005 for a comprehensive review of the literature surrounding this question), but we can lay out some of the issues regarding how technology may reshape the boundaries of the firm (see Lajili and Mahoney 2006 for further recent theoretical discussion). Can technology expand the size of firms through better internal coordination? Perhaps global mega-corporations can instantly coordinate millions of people working on millions of tasks for billions of customers. Or perhaps technology can shrink the firm because of the ability to easily reach so many people in so many markets—imagine millions of small companies Googling one another and using one-click transactions to buy and sell services and products. The answer to both options is "Yes, depending on the circumstances."

Rapid declines in the price of communication have allowed separate parties to interact and coordinate more easily than ever before. Coordination through the use of decentralized information is something we all do without even thinking about it when shopping. The price system is the ultimate example of using decentralized information (Hayek 1945). Consider the number of human beings required to create your morning cup of coffee, from the time that the coffee trees were planted to the time the steaming liquid flows into your cup. The farmer did not need to know how many beans you would need for your cup—he or she just needed to know the market price of beans to know whether to harvest more or less of them. At each stage of production, prices were the coordination mechanism—directing economic actors to send more harvested coffee if prices were high, or to cut back if prices were low. (Imagine the coordination that would be necessary if everything were done by command and control.)

Some researchers have empirically examined the relationship between technology and firm size. Brynjolfsson, Malone, Gurbaxani, and Kambil (1994) empirically demonstrated the impact of information technology on firm size, finding evidence that IT was clearly associated with a *decrease* in employees per establishment. Acemoglu et al. (2007) also analyzed the relationship between the degree of centralization and the adoption of technology. Using data on several thousand French and British firms, they found that firms closer to the technological frontier of their industries were more likely to be decentralized, because top management is less likely to be familiar with newer technology, leading top management to delegate decisions closer to production whereas lower-level managers are likely to be more familiar with the technology.

Colombo and Delmastro (2004), using a sample of roughly 400 Italian manufacturing plants from 1997, produced interesting results about the use of network technology. In the plants with no network technology, the larger the plant size, the more that control was delegated to the plant manager. This makes sense: in a large plant where operations are complex, the plant manager has much better information than those in corporate headquarters. However, for the plants that had adopted network technology, the relationship between plant size and delegation of authority disappeared. With corporate headquarters receiving better information thanks to the network technology, the decision to delegate now depended on factors other than plant size.

Information technology allows one to tackle problems that were previously considered unsolvable. Autor, Levy, and Murnane (2003) used the US Department of Labor's Dictionary of Occupational Titles and constructed a data set of job tasks. They found that, as the US economy transformed over the past few decades, computers had *substituted* for labor for routine tasks, and *complemented* labor for problem-solving or complex tasks. Thus, when working on complicated problems, computers might increase labor demand—and we might expect that firms may grow in size as a result. For example, Microsoft requires tight coordination and collaboration to create its best-selling products, such as Windows and Office. As of June 30, 2008, Microsoft has more than 90,000 employees (source: http://www.microsoft.com)—nearly three times the number of employees it had a decade ago. Suppose that Microsoft were instead broken up into 90,000 sole proprietors. It would seem impossible to write a complex operating system like Windows. Who would make sure that each person was working on the right section of the code, and that they all agreed on what to write?

Yet free software is written by thousands of independent programmers that are still able to achieve coordination. For example, GNU/Linux is written by independent programmers around the world. The source code is open—everyone can look at it and improve any section they choose. Similarly, Wikipedia is a highly successful online encyclopedia with more than 2.9 million articles in English, and more than 100,000 articles in each of 26 other languages (as of June 2009). One of its chief competitors, the venerable *Encyclopedia Britannica*, has a mere 65,000 articles in its print version and 120,000 articles in the online version. Whereas *Britannica* requires a high degree of coordination, Wikipedia is completely decentralized, and anyone can edit virtually any article anytime. The journal *Nature* went so far as to say that Wikipedia was nearly as accurate as *Britannica*. *Britannica*, however, vigorously disputed this claim, and *Nature* issued a response and a point-by-point rebuttal.

Good arguments can be made on both sides. In principle, technology can lead to highly decentralized or to highly centralized firms. Technology can support larger firms or smaller firms. We believe that fruitful research will examine the contexts under which organizations of the future utilize technology to change their organizational structure and size.

productivity resurgence since 1995, and that something unique is occurring in the United States. The further productivity acceleration since 2001 in the absence of substantial investments in IT remains a subject of debate in the literature. Although some explanations focus on the business cycle, our hypothesis is that firms benefited from the organizational capital that they built at the end of the 1990s. We believe that the subsequent drop in 2004–2006 reflects in part the drop in IT investment in 2001–2003, and that the increase in 2007–08 may reflect the pickup in IT investment in 2004. That is, there may be a lag of approximately 3 or 4 years before the process improvements to IT appear in the productivity statistics. Resolving this debate is a promising area for future research.

Further Reading

Erik Brynjolfsson and Lorin Hitt, "Beyond Computation: Information Technology, Organizational Transformation and Business Performance," *Journal of Economic Perspectives* 14 (2000), no. 4: 23–48. Reviews the evidence on how investments in IT are linked with higher productivity and organizational transformation, with an emphasis on firm-level studies.

Council of Economic Advisers, *Economic Report of the President* (Government Printing Office, 2007). Chapter 2 is a useful review of the sources of US productivity growth.

Dale Jorgenson, Mun Ho, and Kevin Stiroh, "A Retrospective Look at the U.S. Productivity Growth Resurgence," *Journal of Economic Perspectives* 22 (2008), no. 1: 3–24. A review of the developments in productivity and projections for future years.

McKinsey Global Institute, *U.S. Productivity Growth 1995–2000: Understanding the Contribution of IT Relative to Other Factors*, 2001. A thorough examination of why productivity accelerated in the United States after 1995.

4   Business Practices That Enhance Productivity

According to the Council of Economic Advisers (2006, p. 37), there is growing evidence that countries with "more flexible, less heavily regulated product and labor markets" are "better able to translate technological advances into productivity gains." Although this may help explain why the United States has recently enjoyed productivity gains not experienced elsewhere, it doesn't explain the large variation in the success of large-scale IT investments at the *firm* level. For example, what explains where firms end up in figure 3.2 above? Or consider table 3.1, which demonstrates the importance of non-IT factors in productivity after 2000.

We begin this chapter by describing seven practices correlated with IT intensity in American companies. According to research conducted over the course of several years at MIT's Center for Digital Business and at the University of Pennsylvania's Wharton School, organizations that adopt

Box 4.1
Seven Pillars of the Digital Organization

Erik Brynjolfsson and Lorin Hitt conducted a large-scale survey of organizational practices and compared the adoption of these practices against other characteristics of the organizations as part of a five-year, $5 million study supported by the National Science Foundation and the MIT Center for Digital Business. The three main findings from the study were as follows: (1) Seven distinct practices were much more common in IT-intensive firms than in their peers. (2) These seven practices were correlated with significant improvements in productivity, in market value, and in other performance metrics. (3) Although not all IT-intensive firms adopted all seven practices, the firms that simultaneously invested in IT and in the practices did disproportionately better than firms that did only one or the other. In other words, the practices are complementary to IT investment.

The seven practices were the following:

1. Move from analog to digital processes   Moving an increasing number of processes into the paperless, digital realm is one of the keys to making productive use of IT. This practice frees the company from the physical limitations of paper and supports the remaining six practices of a digital organization. Digitization also makes it easier to track key performance indicators.

2. Open information access   Restrictive access policies, created by overly protective or possessive managers, can impede the flow of information. Digital organizations, instead, encourage the use of dispersed internal and external information sources. This openness helps both employees and managers do their jobs more productively.

3. Empower the employees   A basic principle of information economics is that information has no economic value if it doesn't change a decision. If employees gain access to more information but lack the authority to make decisions, then the capability is wasted. Digital organizations decentralize authority—pushing decision rights to those with access to information. At the same time, digital business processes complement access and empowerment by helping to enforce business rules or constraints and then alerting appropriate personnel if an exception occurs.

4. Use performance-based incentives   Meritocratic pay structures, incentive pay for individuals and groups, and stock options are common at digital organizations. This contrasts with many traditional companies' use of seniority-based pay, which encourages a sense of paying your dues when an employee is young and enjoying perks and entitlements when he or she is older. The inability of traditional organizations to effectively measure and track the performance of individual employees sometimes leads them to use years-of-service as a proxy for performance.

5. Invest in corporate culture   Part of making productive use of IT is to define and promote a cohesive set of high-level goals and norms that pervade the company. Getting the most out of IT requires some form of cultural cohesion and strategic focus.

6. Recruit the right people   The productivity boost provided by technology is a function of the quality of the people who use it. The fact that technology gives employees more information and authority implies that such employees need to be more capable than those given less individual responsibility.

---

7. Invest in human capital   The preceding six practices all require substantive investment in human capital, but this isn't satisfied by hiring alone. For that reason, digital organizations provide more training than their traditional counterparts. This helps employees operate new digital processes, find information, make decisions, cope with exceptions, meet strategic goals, adhere to cultural norms, set and reach incentive goals, and hire more of the right employees. Many of the changes attendant with becoming a digital organization call for increased levels of thinking and ingenuity on the part of employees.

The results of the study are available at http://digital .mit.edu. The main managerial lessons summarized in this box appeared in Erik Brynjolfsson, "Seven Pillars of Productivity," *Optimize*, May 2005. That article included further details about each pillar and a case study of how Cisco successfully applied these principles in transforming itself into a digital organization.

---

these practices are more productive and have higher market value than their competitors.

Theory of Complementarities: It's Not Just One "Best Practice"[1]

To understand why some firms use IT so much more effectively than others, one must understand the economics of *complementarities*. Milgrom and Roberts (1990) developed a model that delineated the economics of complementarities, and Topkis (1978) is credited with the underlying mathematical framework.

Two practices are complementary if the returns to adopting one practice are greater when the second practice is present. For example, the returns to adopting a certain computer system may be higher in the presence of training than in the absence of training, just as the returns to training may be higher in the presence of the computer system than in its absence (Athey and Stern 1998).

Rather than looking at complements strictly as inputs, Milgrom and Roberts examined *systems* of complementary activities. They demonstrated the chain reaction of business-process redesign that can accompany a change to even one piece of technology. They offered an example of the introduction of CAD/CAM engineering software in manufacturing. CAD/CAM software promotes the use of programmable manufacturing equipment, which makes it possible to offer a broader product line and more frequent production runs. This, in turn, affects marketing, organization, inventory, and output prices. Because customers also value shorter delivery times, the technology that allowed more frequent production runs gives the firm a substantial incentive to reduce other forms of production delays and to invest in computerized ordering systems.

Milgrom and Roberts argued that it is important to adopt systems of complementary activities, rather than adopting one individual "best practice." For instance, they noted that they would not expect to see flexible production equipment used to produce long sequences of identical products (p. 524). Adopting flexible equipment triggers a sequence of other decisions that occur across the firm. The insights of Milgrom and Roberts have been demonstrated by many case studies and empirical papers focusing both on the United States and on other developed countries. We highlight some of them in the next two sections of this chapter.

Case Studies of Complementary Practices

Lincoln Electric, an arc-welding company that began operations in 1895, had not laid off a worker in the United States since 1948, and paid average hourly wages that were double those of its closest competitors (Milgrom and Roberts 1995, p. 200). It paid piece rates—that is, its workers were paid by the amount of output they produced, rather than being paid a fixed salary. Once a piece rate was set, the company remained committed to that rate unless new machines or new production methods were introduced. In addition, the company paid individual annual performance bonuses based on its profits. The bonus typically equaled an employee's regular annual earnings. Given the company's track record, Milgrom and Roberts wondered: If the company's methods have been so widely studied, why hasn't its remarkable success been replicated by other firms?[2] Rather than looking for the answer in the piece rates alone, Milgrom and Roberts hypothesize that it was the *complementarities* inherent in the workplace that made the success of Lincoln Electric so difficult to copy. Copying the practices of paying piece rates may be easy enough, but all the other distinctive features of Lincoln Electric, such as internal ownership, promoting from within, high bonuses, and flexible work rules, are parts of a self-reinforcing system. A system is much more difficult to reproduce than just one or two parts, especially when one considers that many of the important complements, such as corporate culture, may be difficult to accurately observe and even harder to translate to other contexts.

Brynjolfsson, Renshaw, and Van Alstyne (1997) demonstrated the importance of various business processes' fitting together, and the importance of carefully considering the incremental effects of changing workplace practices one at a time, or several at the same time, when evaluating various reengineering efforts. Analyzing the business-process-reengineering efforts of a large medical products company, they attributed the success of the company's efforts to its understanding of the complementarities between its past practices and the practices to which it wanted to transition. Based on this understanding, the company isolated one portion of the factory with a temporary wall to test the new practices and then disseminate them. The company recognized that too many practices would interfere with one another during the transition if it didn't implement them carefully. Brynjolfsson et al. noted how difficult implementing business-process redesign can be—up to 70 percent of business-process-redesign projects fail to accomplish their goals. They cited an instance in which General Motors spent $650 million on upgrading technology in one of its plants in the 1980s. GM did not make any changes to its labor practices, and the new technology did not result in any significant quality or productivity improvements at the plant (Osterman 1991).

Barley (1986) studied the introduction of identical computerized tomography scanners in two different hospitals in the same metropolitan area. They found that the scanners disrupted the relationship between the radiologists and technicians and led to different forms of organization. "Technologies," Barley concluded, "do influence organizational structures in orderly ways, but their influence depends on the specific historical process in which they are embedded. To predict a technology's ramifications for an organization's structure therefore requires a methodology and a conception of technical change open to the construction of grounded, population-specific theories." (p. 107)

Autor, Levy, and Murnane (2002) studied how the introduction of check imaging and optical character recognition technologies affected the reorganization of two floors of a bank branch. Downstairs, in the Deposit Processing Department, image processing led to a substitution of computers for high-school-educated labor. Upstairs, in the Exceptions Processing Department, image processing led to integration of tasks, with "fewer people doing more work in more interesting jobs" (p. 442). The valuable lesson Autor et al. drew from this case study was that the exact same technology, in the same company and in the same building, can have radically different effects on workplace reorganization, depending on human capital and on other non-technology-related factors.

Inspired by the case studies and empowered by the tools developed by Milgrom and Roberts and others, economists have increasingly used statistical methods to formally assess the existence and the size of complementarities in a variety of organizational settings. Most of the studies done so far have focused on complementarities between IT and various organizational practices.

There are two principal ways in which complementarities reveal themselves empirically. First, complementary practices often are correlated with each other. If managers know that training is complementary to IT investments, then training expenditures will tend to be higher when computer expenditures are higher, and vice versa. Second, performance often is higher when complementary practices are adopted together than when they are adopted separately—indeed, this is the definition of complementarity.[3]

In one of the best empirical studies of the relationship between complementarities and productivity, Ichniowski,

Shaw, and Prennushi (1997) used data from 36 steel-finishing lines in 17 different companies and measured the effects of different workplace practices on productivity and product quality. Their main conclusion is that *clusters* of workplace practices have significant and positive effects on productivity, whereas changes in *individual* work practices have little or no effect on productivity (pp. 311–312). Bresnahan, Brynjolfsson, and Hitt (2002) drew similar conclusions from a firm-level analysis of about 300 large American manufacturing and service firms in the years 1987–1994. Studying the organizational complements to technology and their impacts on productivity, they found that "increased use of IT, changes in organizational practices, and changes in products and services *taken together* are the skill-biased technical change[4] that calls for a higher skilled-labor mix" (p. 341). Furthermore, they found that interactions of IT, workplace organization, and human capital are good predictors of productivity.

Brynjolfsson and Hitt (2003) illustrated that complementary investments to IT can take years to come to fruition. Using data from about 500 large firms, they found that the one-year returns to IT were normal, just like ordinary (non-IT) capital. However, they also found that over a longer period (5–7 years) the productivity and output contributions of the same technology investments were up to 5 times as large. They concluded that the dramatic difference in returns was due to the time it took for the complementary investments in human capital and in business-process reorganization to pay off.

Using plant-level data on nearly 800 establishments in the period 1993–1996, Black and Lynch (2004) examined the relationship between productivity and human-resource practices. "Workplace organization, including reengineering, teams, incentive pay and employee voice," they asserted, "have been a significant component of the turnaround in productivity growth in the US during the 1990s" (p. F97). In a related paper, Black and Lynch (2001) examined how workplace practices, IT, and human capital affect productivity. Using data on about 600 manufacturing plants from the years 1987–1993, they found that adopting a Total Quality Management system alone did not meaningfully affect productivity. However, they found that plants that extended profit-sharing programs to production workers, included more employees in decision making, or had more computer usage by production workers showed significantly higher productivity.

Bartel, Ichniowski, and Shaw's (2007) analysis of 212 valve-manufacturing plants is an excellent example of how IT investments are affecting business strategies and innovation. Bartel et al. found that plants that adopted IT had shorter setup times in production, and had customized production in smaller runs, rather than using longer batches. The study found that increased use of IT also leads to the adoption of new workplace practices and raises the demand for more skilled workers.

There has been much debate about why productivity growth has been higher in the United States than in Europe. (See O'Mahony and van Ark 2003 for a good review of the literature.) One argument explains the difference in terms of factors external to the firm, such as taxes, regulation, and culture. Another argument is that, for a variety of reasons, there will be differences in how firms organize themselves from country to country.

Two recent papers suggest that differences in productivity between the United Kingdom and the United States may be due to the organizational design of firms or to firm-specific IT-related intangible assets that are often excluded in macroeconomic growth accounting exercises. These papers aim to compare the differences between US-owned and UK-owned firms operating in the United Kingdom. The authors of these papers attempt to answer the question of whether there is something unique about US *ownership*—as opposed to being located on US soil (where there is less regulation and stronger product market competition)—that leads to higher productivity growth.

Crespi, Criscuolo, and Haskel (2007) presented evidence that US-owned firms operating in the United Kingdom implemented more productivity-enhancing business practices than their UK-owned counterparts. Their study, based on data from approximately 6,000 British firms across all industries in the period 1998–2000, used a variable as a proxy for complementary organizational assets. Crespi et al. found that IT had high returns when organizational factors were omitted in the analysis. However, when they included the organizational proxy variable, the returns attributed to IT were lower, which suggests that some of the IT-related boost in productivity came from organizational factors. In other words, something unique occurs when human capital and other workplace practices are combined with technology. Yet Crespi et al. found "no additional impact on productivity growth from the interaction of organizational capital and non-IT investment" (p. 2). These findings were consistent with recent literature. Their main contribution was their finding that organizational change was affected by ownership and market competition, and that US-owned firms operating in the United Kingdom were more likely to introduce organizational change than non-US-owned (and non-UK-owned) firms, which were more likely to introduce organizational change than UK-owned firms (p. 3). Bloom, Sadun, and Van Reenen (2007) conducted a similar study of 8,000 establishments across all industries in the United Kingdom from 1995 to 2003. They found that US-owned establishments were more productive than UK-owned or other foreign-owned companies operating in the United Kingdom. They specifically attributed this difference to the use of IT-related organizational capital.[5]

Bugamelli and Pagano (2004), using data on about 1,700 Italian manufacturing firms, found "a delay of at least 7 years in ICT adoption with respect to the USA" (p. 2275). They rejected the notion that the gap was due to sectoral specialization of the Italian economy into industries such as textiles, clothing, and food, which are not as IT-intensive. Rather, they argue that the absence of complementary business reorganization was the barrier to investment in IT in Italy.

Caroli and Van Reenen (2001) studied the organizational characteristics of British and French establishments in 1984 and 1990 (UK) and in 1992 (France) and generated three major findings. One was that organizational changes led to less demand for unskilled workers. A second was that a higher cost of skills led to a lower probability of organizational change. A third was that organizational change led to faster productivity growth in firms with more skilled workers than in firms with fewer skilled workers.

Summary

Major empirical and case studies from the period 1995–2008 point to business-process reorganization as a major factor in explaining productivity differences across plants or firms. Because of the important firm-specific factors involved, these studies go beyond what can be explained by industry data. Further, these studies together can help explain why productivity accelerated more in the United States than in Europe.

Further Reading

Nicholas Bloom, Raffaella Sadun, and John Van Reenen, *Americans Do I.T. Better: U.S. Multinationals and the Productivity Miracle*, NBER Working Paper 13085, 2007. Addresses the question of why American firms have been more productive than their European counterparts. Focuses on whether the high productivity of American firms is due to their being located in the United States or to their being US-owned regardless of location.

Erik Brynjolfsson, Amy Austin Renshaw, and Marshall Van Alstyne, "The Matrix of Change," *Sloan Management Review* 38 (1997), no. 2: 37–54. An insightful case study into how interactions between old and new workplace practices can interfere with organizational change.

Robert Gibbons, "Four Formal(izable) Theories of the Firm?" *Journal of Economic Behavior & Organization* 58 (2005), no. 2: 200–245. Reviews four major theories of the firm and integrates them into one framework.

Casey Ichniowski, Kathryn Shaw, and Giovanna Prennushi, "The Effects of Human Resource Management Practices on Productivity: A Study of Steel Finishing Lines," *American Economic Review* 87 (1997), no. 3: 291–313. A thorough and rigorous empirical paper that demonstrates the relationship between human-resources practices and productivity.

Paul Milgrom and John Roberts, "Complementarities and Fit: Strategy, Structure, and Organizational Change in Manufacturing," *Journal of Accounting and Economics* 19 (1995), no. 2–3: 179–208. Begins with a theoretical discussion of complementarities, then applies this theory to a case study of Lincoln Electric.

5   Organizational Capital

While the studies in chapter 4 document the complementarities between technology and workplace practices, we believe the next step is to conceptualize these practices as an asset, which we call organizational capital. We like to think of a firm's organizational capital as its stock of nontradable intangible assets, which conceptually have some similarities to physical assets. The intangible stock of assets takes time to develop, because, by definition, it cannot be bought on the market. Dierickx and Cool (1989, p. 1510) defined these kinds of assets as "nontradeable, nonimitable, and nonsubstitutable." A successful company may have taken years to build its intangible asset stock to what it is today. Firms can either build up their intangible capital assets by making complementary investments or drain them by not continually innovating and redesigning their business processes as they become outdated.

Measuring intangible assets has important implications for management, because we often see that high-performance organizations are the organizations that measure themselves best. If better measurement of intangibles indicated their large quantity or suggested large returns, organizations would be encouraged to invest more in this kind of capital.

The definition and measurement of organizational capital is an emerging research area within economics. Organizational capital can include such practices as the allocation of decision rights, the design of incentive systems, cumulative investments in training and skill developments, and even supplier and customer networks. Although gross domestic product measures the production of innovative products, such as a new generation of mobile phones, GDP does not directly measure the creation of innovative businesses processes. We believe that organizational capital encompasses the changes wrought by these innovative business processes. At this point, although there is no consensus on how to define organizational capital, there are two good surveys of the nascent literature. One is by Black and Lynch (2005), who propose a definition of organizational capital that comprises three components: workforce training, employee voice, and work design. The other is by Ichniowski and Shaw (2003), who review several studies documenting innovative work practices and then describe their preferred research approach to measuring organizational capital: the "insider econometrics" approach. In this approach, the researcher identifies a narrow production process and conducts field research to understand this process thoroughly. Then the researcher gathers data from sites where this process has been used over a number of years and performs a wider econometric analysis. Bartel, Ichniowski, and Shaw (2007) used the latter method.

How Accounting Rules Misclassify Investment in Organizational Capital

Accounting rules are not designed to measure investment in organizational capital. For example, although direct investment in hardware or software is often measured, it is just one small part of the total contribution that computers make to the workplace. When a company makes a large investment in technology designed to integrate various databases and other organizational processes, such as an Enterprise Resource Planning (ERP) system, most of the startup costs do not come from the hardware or software investments themselves. In a typical $20 million ERP installation, only $4 million is spent on hardware and software combined, while $16 million is spent on organization (Gormley et al. 1998). The bulk of these organizational costs can be attributed to reorganization and training. Installing an ERP system could mean taking a hundred databases that had operated independently and linking them tightly together into a new system.

Furthermore, ERP systems are not easy to customize: A firm has to catalog hundreds if not thousands of its separate business processes in order to properly customize the software. One manager of an ERP implementation with whom we spoke (at MIT) considered this a virtue. His reasoning was that this would force departments with disparate methods of accounting to standardize on a single method: the one already embedded in the ERP system that was being rolled out.

Under typical accounting rules, most of the $4 million spent on hardware and software is counted as investment and depreciated over a number of years, whereas most of the $16 million is typically "expensed"—that is, deducted in the first year. According to Statement of Position 98–1 of the American Institute of Certified Public Accountants (AICPA), only costs incurred during the application development stage of a software project, such as coding, testing, and installing, can be counted as investment—in other words, they can be capitalized. In contrast, all preliminary development costs (such as hiring consultants to help make a strategic decision about starting an IT project) and post-implementation costs (such as the cost of training) must be expensed. For small projects, firms have the discretion to expense instead of capitalize. For instance, at FleetBoston Financial software projects smaller than $500,000 were normally expensed in their entirety (Brynjolfsson, Hitt, and Yang 2002, p. 148). We think of these associated costs as investments in organizational

capital, not as expenses. For example, intangible investments were very important at Dell Inc., which "combined
new materials management software with a set of rede-
signed workflows to roughly halve the floor space in its
main server assembly plant, while increasing overall
throughput and reducing work-in-process inventories"
(ibid., pp. 146–147). This reorganization can be thought of
as creating an intangible asset, which provided the
company just as much—if not more—benefit than another
physical plant. This know-how can theoretically be scaled
without limits, whereas the physical plant will be able to
generate value only until it has reached its full capacity.
As is the case with physical capital assets, we consider
organizational capital to be an asset variable.

Unlike adding to the stock of physical capital assets,
increasing the stock of organizational capital assets
through business-process reengineering is very hard.
Michael Hammer articulated the difficulties of business-
process reengineering quite well: "Reengineering cannot
be planned meticulously and accomplished in small and
cautious steps. It's an all-or-nothing proposition with an
uncertain result." (1990, p. 105) As to why more businesses do not take the necessary steps to innovate,
Hammer remarked that "at the heart of reengineering is
the notion of discontinuous thinking—of recognizing and
breaking away from outdated rules and fundamental
assumptions that underlie operations" (p. 107). In the case
study of the medical products company discussed in the

previous chapter (Brynjolfsson, Renshaw, and Van Alstyne 1997), breaking old routines was quite difficult, even though the company had a specific plan it wanted to implement. The difficulty stemmed from interference between old and new practices.

Possible Methods of Estimating Organizational Capital

Efforts to reengineer business processes, to create more IT-intensive business practices, and to reinvent organizations go almost unseen and unmeasured by most economists and policy makers. The Bureau of Economic Analysis, entrusted with keeping the official GDP statistics of the United States, releases estimates of traditional research and development spending going back to 1959. In fact, the BEA has recently begun to publish a set of parallel GDP accounts that treat R&D as an investment rather than an expense, and plans to fully incorporate R&D investment in the core accounts by 2013 (Aizcorbe et al. 2009). But what we are talking about here—experimentation with new forms of business, or R&D for business processes—is not measured as formally.

In the literature we have found some basic methods with which to estimate intangibles. One is to estimate spending directly, either at the macroeconomic level or at the firm level. Another is to use the financial markets, and to estimate intangibles by comparing the total market value of a firm's assets against the value of the firm's tangible assets. Yet a third method uses analysts' estimates of a firm's earnings to construct the value of intangibles.

In table 5.1, to illustrate one attempt to measure intangible investment in the US economy, we reproduce an estimate from Corrado, Hulten, and Sichel (2005, 2006). Corrado et al. classify intangible investments into three broad categories and identify how these are treated in the National Income and Product Accounts (NIPAs). They also aggregate various macroeconomic sources to estimate the value of annual investment in this intangible capital. The first two categories, Computerized Information and Innovative Property, relatively speaking, are better captured in the national accounts than the third category, Economic Competencies.[1] In that category, firm spending is not counted as investment in the NIPAs. The sum of these intangibles is impressive: about $1.2 trillion per year on average from 2000 to 2003, with nearly $1 trillion of that not counted as investment. The size of this uncounted investment is nearly as large as what is counted as investment—which was $1.1 trillion per year during this period.

Another method that can be used to estimate the size of intangibles is to poll firms directly, asking them how much they invest in training, organizational change, and other intangible complements when they install or upgrade technology. Figure 5.1 shows the results from

Table 5.1
Intangible capital and its treatment in the National Income and Product Accounts. Sources: Corrado et al. 2005, p. 23; Corrado et al. 2006, p. 40.

	Type of knowledge capital	Current status in national income and product accounts	Estimated annual average expenditure (2000–2003) (billions of dollars)
Computerized information	Knowledge embedded in computer programs and computerized databases	Major component, computer software, is capitalized	172.5
Innovative property	Knowledge acquired through scientific R&D and nonscientific inventive and creative activities	Most spending for new product discovery and development is expensed[a]	230.5 (scientific R&D);237.2 (nonscientific R&D)
Economic competencies	Knowledge embedded in firm-specific human and structural resources, including brand names	No items recognized as assets of the firm	160.8 (brand equity):425.1 (firm-specific resources)
Total			1,226.2, of which $977.7 billion is not counted in the NIPA as investment[b]

a. Two small components—oil and gas exploration, and architectural and engineering services embedded in structures and equipment purchases—are included in the NIPA as business fixed investment.
b. Average annual NIPA business fixed investment was $1,141.9 billion.

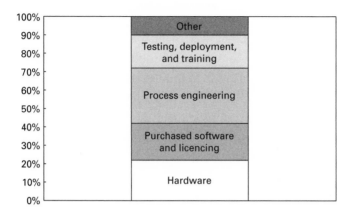

Figure 5.1
Percent of costs of IT projects at large manufacturing firms. Source:
Brynjolfsson, Fitoussi, and Hitt 2006.

one such survey. The data were taken from a sample of
large manufacturing firms. This figure demonstrates that
hardware accounts for only one-fifth of the costs of such
large-scale enterprise projects as Enterprise Resource
Planning, Customer Relationship Management, and
Supply Chain Management.

Brynjolfsson, Hitt, and Yang (2002) used data on the
securities market to document the existence of organizational capital that is highly complementary to technology
investments. The data set combined human resource practice data, computer data, and financial data, such as assets,
equity, and debt for several hundred large firms. Whereas
a dollar of non-IT capital (whether physical, such as the
value of buildings, or non-physical, such as accounts

receivable) was associated with roughly a dollar of market value, a dollar of computer capital was associated with more than $10 of market value. Including a measure of organizational practices in the analysis changed the results dramatically. While a dollar of computer assets in the presence of a cluster of workplace practices (such as self-managed teams and decentralized decision rights) was valued at $10 or more by the market, a dollar of computer assets in firms without these complementary practices was worth much closer to $1. This interaction was specific to computer capital. Ordinary (non-IT) capital and other assets were worth about $1 in the market whether or not the firms had this cluster of practices. Figure 5.2, adapted from this study, illustrates this finding. Having either high IT or a cluster of distinct "digital organization" practices alone is not worth nearly as much as having them together.

Financial-market estimates also have been used to develop measures of organizational capital. Cummins (2005) used financial markets but departed from previous models that treated intangible capital like tangible capital in a production function. Instead, Cummins constructed the value of the firm as the present value of analysts' earnings estimates. Lev and Radhakrishnan (2005) developed a model of organizational capital and found that this capital was highly correlated with IT assets. They also found that analysts had underestimated the value of this capital, probably because it is so difficult to directly observe.

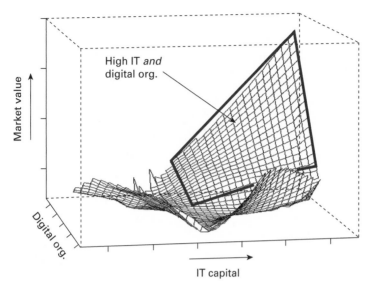

High IT *and* digital org.

IT capital

Figure 5.2
Market value as a function of IT assets and digital business processes. Adapted from Brynjolfsson, Hitt, and Yang 2002. Data are from several hundred large firms. IT capital data are from Computer Intelligence Corp. The variable labeled "Digital org." was constructed from surveys the authors conducted and then standardized to mean 0 and variance 1. Source of market-value data: Compustat.

Theoretical Models of Organizational Capital and Growth

The effect of organizational capital on economic growth and the degree to which national accounts might under-estimate the value of intangible capital in the economy have been examined in a number of studies. Oliner, Sichel, and Stiroh (2007) used growth accounting and explicitly incorporated IT-related intangibles in an effort to explain the difference between the 1995–2000 and post-2000 productivity resurgences. Nakamura (2003) estimated that US firms invested $1 trillion annually in intangible assets, and that the total stock of intangible assets was roughly $5 trillion. Atkeson and Kehoe (2005) claimed that the total payment to owners of manufacturing firms from organizational capital is more than one-third of the total payouts they receive from physical capital. They also asserted that "the total payments that owners of manufacturing firms receive from all intangible capital in the US National Income and Product Accounts" are "about 8 percent of manufacturing output" (p. 1027), and that payments to organizational capital constitute about 40 percent of those payments. Oulton and Srinivasan (2005) estimated the effect of technology-related organizational capital in the United Kingdom on multi-factor productivity (MFP) growth and argued that the unmeasured organizational capital in the United Kingdom could have lowered official MFP estimates. Yang and Brynjolfsson (2001) presented a detailed model that proposed revising the NIPAs by taking into account previously uncounted intangible assets. They estimated that the US economy had grown 1 percentage point faster per year in the 1990s than the official statistics indicated, because of omitted intangible capital.

Summary

Although definitions and methods vary, the literature agrees on one basic point: the size of the total stock of intangible capital in the United States is very large—as much as several trillion dollars. Often this capital does not show up in balance sheets or economic figures, either in government accounts or as an item in firm-level balance sheets. Estimating the value of this capital in a definitive way, and using it in models of economic growth, is an opportunity to help managers make more effective investments.

Further Reading

Ann Bartel, Casey Ichniowski, and Kathryn Shaw, "How Does Information Technology Affect Productivity? Plant-Level Comparisons of Product Innovation, Process Improvement, and Worker Skills," *Quarterly Journal of Economics* 122 (2007), no. 4: 1721–1758. A detailed study documenting how IT led to process changes in the valve-manufacturing industry.

Erik Brynjolfsson, Lorin Hitt, and Shinkyu Yang, "Intangible Assets: Computers and Organizational Capital," *Brookings Papers on Economic Activity* 1 (2002): 137–198. The authors demonstrate that it is the combination of IT and organizational practices that is associated with higher market value, rather than either one alone.

Carol Corrado, Charles Hulten, and Daniel Sichel, *Intangible Capital and Economic Growth*, Working Paper 2006-24, Finance and Economics Discussion Series, Divisions of Research & Statistics and Monetary Affairs, Federal Reserve Board, 2006. The authors revise the standard growth accounting model to explicitly incorporate the use of intangible capital.

Stephen Oliner, Daniel Sichel, and Kevin Stiroh, "Explaining a Productive Decade," *Brookings Papers on Economic Activity* 38 (2007), no. 1: 81–152. The authors develop a model to incorporate IT-related intangible investment in a standard growth accounting model.

John Roberts, *The Modern Firm: Organizational Design for Performance and Growth* (Oxford University Press, 2004). An eminently readable book that combines case studies and economic theory.

6 Incentives for Innovation in the Information Economy

Debate about copyright laws, patents, and intellectual property has escalated in recent years because of the improved ability to replicate and distribute digital information. Lower distribution costs greatly increase the potential rewards to successful innovation and yet may also adversely affect the incentives to innovate because of rapid imitation or even piracy. Before we look at the factors affecting the incentive to innovate, let us look at the difficulties of even measuring this knowledge input and output in the first place.

Difficulties Measuring Input and Output in Knowledge Industries

Anyone can visit one of the thousands of Starbucks locations in the United States and find out the price of a cup of coffee, a latte, or a pound of beans. These are tangible goods, and the market for them is readily assessed.

Similarly, some service industries have straightforward measurements of prices and quantities sold. For example, the government has detailed data on the number of seats sold on airplanes, or the revenue generated from hotel rooms. Valuing knowledge, however, is difficult. We cannot measure it directly, and we have the dual problem of measuring both price and quantity.

According to one estimate (Lyman and Varian 2003), the amount of information produced in 2002 was about 5 exabytes, equivalent to 37,000 times the information in the Library of Congress. In comparison with tangible goods, there are virtually no limits on how far information can travel or how many times it can be used. In most cases, one person's enjoyment does not diminish another's enjoyment of the same information. In other words, information is a non-rival good. In contrast, when one person consumes a rival good (such as a cup of coffee), another person cannot. For every keyword search, for example, there can be a variety of effects throughout the economy. For instance, a consumer might find information in Wikipedia that helps her plan a vacation trip, or might view an entertaining YouTube video. Similarly, through a Google search, Accenture might find information that allows it to write a report for UPS. Now multiply these possibilities by the more than 8 billion searches done per month in the United States,[2] and the cumulative potential value of these searches, both to consumers and businesses, could be tremendous. But we simply don't know what that value is at the moment. The free information that is produced and available online is not counted as output in the national accounts. This leads to an underestimate of labor productivity (output per hours worked). To the extent that this output is uncounted, the economy will not appear to be as productive as it really is.

In markets for physical goods, the market prices of inputs such as coffee beans or the hourly wage of a barista are relatively straightforward to compute. Measuring input in information markets is another matter, however, because the inputs may consist of unpriced information goods or intangibles. Furthermore, there may have to be a combination of several intangible sources in order to create something valuable. Suppose some people get together to create a piece of software, a legal brief, or a movie. Because of teamwork and collaboration, the time each person works on a product is not necessarily going to be directly related to the value of the output. Pricing an individual contribution in an information market can be a difficult task.

Producers (and consumers) of information goods encounter two major problems when it comes to pricing information. First, information is an experience good, so buyers don't know how much they will like a research report (for example) until they have read it. But by then they have already paid for it. This makes buyers unlikely to be willing to pay the full value of information goods, so producers can't charge a price that reflects their full value. Second, because the marginal cost of digital information is essentially zero, standard markup pricing techniques, such as taking the marginal cost and adding 40 percent, won't work.

One way producers of information goods can mitigate the problem of pricing individual pieces of knowledge is to bundle the pieces together and charge one price for the whole package. This is a common strategy. Research databases charge a flat fee price to libraries, cable TV operators offer packages of channels for a single monthly charge, and online music services offer one price to listen to millions of songs. It can be a lot easier to predict demand for a group of goods than for any one good. It is also more difficult to compete against a bundle as an individual seller of information goods. There is a growing literature on the strategic advantage of bundling zero-marginal-cost information goods to capture a greater share of the market (Bakos and Brynjolfsson 1999, 2000; Nalebuff 2004).

But how would a bundler fairly compensate the individual artists in a music bundle if the music is only sold together and not a la carte? Brynjolfsson and Zhang (2007) describe one possible method to value an individual's input to a bundle of information goods. The idea is to give consumers digital "coupons." Suppose that a small, randomly selected group of consumers of a music bundle are offered coupons if they are willing to forgo certain songs that are included in the bundle. If the coupon amounts are selected randomly, say between \$1 and \$10, the content distributor can see how changing the price of keeping a particular song in the bundle affects the number of people willing to forgo the song. Using this information, the

Box 6.1
General-Purpose Technologies

If all technological progress in the economy stopped today, would productivity growth grind to a halt? We don't think so. On the contrary, we believe that there are decades' worth of potential innovations to be made by creatively combining inventions that we already have in creative ways. For instance, if you combine Google Maps, GPS technology, cell phone technology, and restaurant reviews, you get the ability to find the closest Thai restaurant to your location and get its Zagat rating. None of these inputs is necessarily new, but combining them can result in a significant improvement over using them separately. This illustrates what researchers call a *general-purpose technology*, meaning a technology that might be used in many different ways.

David and Wright (2003, p. 144) listed the following criteria for a general-purpose technology, based on the definition proposed by Lipsey, Bekar, and Carlaw (1998):

• wide scope for improvement and elaboration

• applicability across a broad range of uses

• potential for use in a wide variety of products and processes

• strong complementarities with existing or potential technologies.

Computing isn't the only example of a general-purpose technology. Bresnahan and Trajtenberg (1995) developed a model of the use of semiconductors as a general-purpose technology, characterized by "pervasiveness, inherent potential for technical improvements, and 'innovational complementarities'" (p. 83). As semiconductors became cheaper to produce, they created downstream sectors, which fed the demand for more semiconductors, which fed more demand downstream, and so on.

On one level, computing can make existing processes run faster. But a more exciting use of computing would be to push out the invention-possibility frontier. Computing can change the way business is done. As a historical example of this principle David (1990) described the invention of the dynamo and its effect on the organization of the factory. His main point was that decades passed before factories reorganized themselves internally and made truly significant productivity gains possible. David saw the history of electrification as a lesson for computing. It took the 1970s, the 1980s, and part of the 1990s for businesses to fully transform their business processes to make the most effective use of computing. David's argument, made during the "productivity paradox" years, was ahead of its time.

content distributor can trace a demand curve for individual songs within the bundle. Using these demand curves, the bundler can then compensate each of the artists accordingly.

Knowledge Spillovers

Who pays for knowledge creation? How does knowledge flow through the economy? Who benefits from created knowledge? Wassily Leontief won a Nobel Prize in 1973 for his pioneering work in using input-output (I-O) matrices to trace the flows of commodities in the US economy. As an example, we can analyze the coffee industry using I-O matrices. We can start with the agriculture industry, which harvests the beans, and then proceed to manufacturing, which makes instant coffee, or to retail, which sells cups of coffee to consumers. The output of one firm passes to the next firm as an input, and so processes follow in a linear fashion from growing the beans to drinking the brew. But information does not follow a linear chain throughout the economy. Because the same idea or piece of information can be used by more than one person or firm once it is created, there is a phenomenon called *knowledge spillovers*.

The nature of knowledge spillovers means that the private return for creating knowledge will be less than the social return. Let us illustrate this with a numerical example. Suppose a certain piece of information about improving a business process would cost a company $10 million to create. This could be the value of the time management spends thinking about the problem, or it could be a fee paid to an outside consultant. And suppose that the information will yield a return of only $2 million in sales to the company. Seeing that the costs are much greater than the benefits, the company will not undertake the investment. Now suppose that this piece of information could add significant value to other firms in the economy without hurting the first firm—in other words, it is non-rival. Maybe the cumulative value of this information to all firms in the economy is $100 million. From a social perspective, everyone would be better off if the first firm invested in the new piece of knowledge. The social return is a profit of $90 million. But the private loss to the company creating the information is $8 million. The misalignment of the social and private returns leads to chronic under-investment in R&D by the private sector. Part of this shortfall can be addressed by government support for R&D through channels such as National Science Foundation grants. But as more of the economy becomes knowledge based, we need to think about creating incentives so that more firms continue to invest in knowledge.

A number of scholars have studied the effects of R&D spillovers. In the classic paper, Griliches (1958) examined the social rate of return to research activity as opposed to just the private rate of return. Jaffe et al. (1993) found significant geographical spillovers in patent citations in their study of US firms. When analyzing the citation of previous patents in firms' patent applications, they found that, after controlling for other factors, the cited patents were 5–10 times more likely to come from other firms in the same metropolitan area. Cameron's 1998 survey of the literature finds that R&D spillovers are persistent and robust to a variety of different measures, such as patent matrices or input-output tables (p. 8). Cameron concludes that R&D spillovers between countries do not account for most of the productivity growth in a mature economy. Rather, it is the domestic spillovers that account for most growth. One reason is that it takes considerable effort to exploit the results of foreign research. Another is that culture, geography, and secrecy make knowledge harder to diffuse across international borders. Third, R&D in universities create large spillovers locally (p. 22).

Yet knowledge spillovers may also reduce returns to the original producer. What happens to the incentives to innovate when a movie can be perfectly copied and distributed to the public even before it is released in theaters? Previously, making copies entailed either a high cost or a loss of quality, so that the original item still had a premium value. This is not so today.

The flip side of costless copies is that the Internet has made it easier than ever to distribute content and to create a vast amount of value for millions of people. Why do football players make more money, on average, than hockey players? In a word, television. Today the least valuable National Football League team is worth about as much as the two most valuable National Hockey League franchises combined. The NFL receives nearly $4 billion per year in TV revenues and shares it among the teams, so that each team receives more than $100 million. In fact, television accounts for two-thirds of the NFL's revenue. The NHL's TV contract with Comcast's Versus Network, however, was for $72.5 million for the 2007–08 season, with inflationary increases through 2010.

Disruptive Technologies: Are Low-Cost Copies a Boon, or a Bane?

On one hand, the Internet makes it possible for content creators to produce enormous potential value for millions of consumers, because it lets creators reach many people easily. On the other hand, if content prices drop to zero as a result of widespread copying, revenues will also drop to zero, regardless of the volume. Which effect will be more powerful? Below we offer three historical examples of information industries that, although confronted with declining distribution costs, have not only survived but thrived.

Libraries vs. Book Publishers
Shapiro and Varian (1999) detailed the history of lending libraries in England (pp. 94–95) and demonstrated that publishers were able to make more money. In 1800, there were only 80,000 regular readers in all of England. But the

introduction of the romance novel fueled an explosion in book sales, and bookstores became for-profit libraries by renting out books because they could not keep up with demand. Book publishers were worried that the libraries would hurt their business. Shapiro and Varian cite Charles Knight (1854, p. 284): "[W]hen circulating libraries were first opened, the booksellers were much alarmed; and their rapid increase added to their fears, and led them to think that the sale of books would be much diminished by such libraries." Instead, the opposite happened. The number of readers in England grew from 80,000 in 1800 to over 5 million in 1850. Shapiro and Varian conclude: "[I]t was the presence of the circulating libraries that killed the old publishing model, but at the same time it created a new business model of mass-market books. The for-profit circulating libraries continued to survive well into the 1950s. What killed them off was not a lack of interest in reading but rather the paperback book—an even cheaper way of providing literature to the masses." (p. 95)

Photocopiers vs. Journals

Liebowitz (1985) found that photocopying did not harm the profits of academic journals. In the early days of photocopying, publishers worried that photocopying was hurting journals' profits. Why would individuals subscribe to journals if they could go to the library and photocopy what they needed? However, Liebowitz concluded that because each journal could now be used by more people within a given library, journals would be more valuable to libraries. Until the invention of the photocopier, almost all journals used to charge the same subscription fees to individuals and libraries. Using data from 80 economics journals from 1959 (when the photocopier was invented) through 1982, Liebowitz found that journals began to charge libraries more for subscriptions than they charged individuals, and credited this to photocopying. He also found that publishers raised the prices of journals that were frequently photocopied more than they raised the prices of those that were photocopied less often.[3] By doing this, the journals did not have to try to extract a photocopying fee from individual users. Instead, the revenue was indirectly appropriated from the libraries.

Videocassette Recorders vs. Hollywood

Shapiro and Varian (1999) note that in the 1980s the Hollywood studios felt threatened by the early video rental stores, but that it was soon clear that the studios made more money because of such stores. As the price of a video-cassette recorder dropped from $1,000 to less than $200, the studios lowered the prices of movies on video tape from $90 in 1980 to as low as $10 in the late 1980s. Demand increased dramatically (as one would expect with 80–90 percent price declines), and the studios made far greater profits than they had before the introduction of the VCR.

Innovative Business Models

Disruptive technologies have forced innovation in the ways companies do business. Companies that don't innovate are driven out of business, but the returns to companies that do innovate are much larger than before. With each successive innovation in communication technology, the ability to reach more people easily has increased exponentially. If more people can enjoy a service, more value is created and thus more value will accrue to the winners.

We can imagine a day in the near future when the compact disc as a medium for music is replaced entirely by electronic versions, or a day when physical books are replaced by e-books. Insofar as books and music are two of the most important products that Amazon sells, should Amazon be worried that it will go out of business? Not according to Jeff Wilke, Amazon's Senior Vice President for North American Retail, who told us in 2006: "As music becomes digital, our customers will need something to listen to it with. They will need headphones and iPods. When books become digital, they will need portable e-book readers and accessories to read them. As long as it can fit into a box, we can store it in our warehouse and ship it to them." In addition, Amazon has become increasingly active as a purveyor of e-books, e-documents, and movies (via Amazon Kindle and Video On Demand), and it often lists various media options for the same content within same product page.

As a lesson in what can happen to a producer of information when it fails to innovate its business model in light of lower communication and replication costs, Shapiro and Varian (1999) cited the fact that in 1986 the telephone company Nynex made New York City's telephone directory available on a CD and sold it for $10,000 a copy. Shapiro and Varian noted that "the Nynex executive in charge of the product . . . left to set up his own company, Pro CD, to produce a national directory," and "[a] consultant who worked on the project had the same idea and created Digital Directory Assistance" (p. 23). As more companies entered the market, the price of the CD dropped from $10,000 to a few hundred dollars and then to nearly nothing. The mathematician Joseph Bertrand would have predicted that outcome more than 100 years ago. Firms that compete in commodity markets will see the price of their goods driven down to marginal cost. In the case of the New York telephone book, the marginal cost of another disc is close to zero, so we would expect the price to be competed down close to zero. However, to the extent that content providers differentiate themselves through non-price attributes such as reputation, price will not be driven down to zero.

Persistent Price Dispersion Online

"Price dispersion," the economist George Stigler once wrote, "is a manifestation—and, indeed, it is the measure of ignorance in the market." (1961, p. 214) Today, the Internet makes it easy to compare prices. It is easy to think that prices should be driven to the same value, and that as a result all profit margins would vanish. Several researchers have tested this theory using online book markets.

Every book published in the United States has an International Standard Book Number, which uniquely identifies it. As in the Nynex example cited above, the conventional wisdom held that Bertrand-style price competition would drive the price of a book down to its marginal cost, and profits would disappear. According to this line of thought, Amazon should have been driven out of business long ago, because as soon as another website came along offering a book for even 10 cents less, everyone should have flocked to that site. But that hasn't happened. Brynjolfsson and Smith (2000) noted that in their study the Internet bookseller with the lowest price had lower prices than Amazon 99 percent of the time. Yet Amazon has obtained its large market share because consumers value its reputation for customer satisfaction and service. Chevalier and Goolsbee (2003) found that Amazon commanded a significant premium in the market over even a well-known rival such as Barnes & Noble (bn.com). We believe that, if anything, brand matters *more* online than in the real world. To see why, contrast buying a book online to buying a book in a store. In the store, you can examine a book to your heart's content, and once you pay for it you have it. If you purchase a book online, however, you have to trust that it will be delivered, on time, in the condition in which you thought it would be. Price search engines such as Froogle have armed consumers with more data than ever before about prices, but consumers are willing to pay a premium to a company whose service and reputation they trust.

Summary

Although decreasing communications costs have been affecting incentives for innovation for centuries, free and perfect copies that are easy to distribute were never possible until recently. But the Internet, so far, has not killed innovation. Rather, it has created an entire generation of individual innovators. Every day, YouTube delivers hundreds of millions of video streams, most of them generated by users. If history is any guide, the Internet will encourage vast amounts of innovation. The real questions are "Who will the winners be?" and "What mechanisms will be used to compensate them?"

Further Reading

Erik Brynjolfsson and Xiaoquan (Michael) Zhang, "Innovation Incentives for Information Goods," in *Innovation Policy and the Economy*, volume 7, ed. A. Jaffe et al. (MIT Press, 2007). A discussion of the special problems associated with providing incentives for the creators of information goods (software, music, books, movies) that can be reproduced at nearly zero marginal cost.

Demonstrates how bundling combined with a "couponing mechanism" for assessing value could solve this dilemma.

Judith Chevalier and Austan Goolsbee, "Measuring Prices and Price Competition Online: Amazon.com and BarnesandNoble.com," *Quantitative Marketing and Economics* 1 (2003), no. 2: 203–222. An empirical study that demonstrates that brand—and not just the lowest price—matters on the Internet.

Paul David, "The Dynamo and the Computer: An Historical Perspective on the Modern Productivity Paradox," *American Economic Review* 80 (1990), no. 2: 355–361. An instructive example of how long it took for the dynamo to revolutionize the factory floor. The comparison is to computers, which have similarly taken decades to "appear in the productivity statistics."

Carl Shapiro and Hal Varian, *Information Rules: A Strategic Guide to the Network Economy* (Harvard Business School Press, 1999). An excellent and accessible overview of the economics of information goods.

7   Consumer Surplus

At the beginning of 1913, there were 7,456,074 telephones in operation in the United States, less than one for every 13 people.[1] About 10 percent of roads were surfaced,[2] and only one person in 80 owned a registered motor vehicle.[3] Telephones and cars were too expensive for all but the exceptionally wealthy. (Remember, a Reo cost $1,095 in 1913, about 3 times the average person's income.) Today, of course, nearly every household in the United States has a telephone (and/or a mobile phone). There are more than 243 million privately registered motor vehicles in the country—about one for every 1.2 people.[4]

By traditional measures of input and output, information technology appears to be a relatively small part of the economy. The technologies behind the products that have made life easier, safer, healthier, or more comfortable are of tremendous value to society but are not counted in government measures. However, economists have been thinking for decades about one measure that may help us determine the value of technological innovation in our economy. It is *consumer surplus.*

Estimating Consumer Surplus

Consumer surplus is the aggregate net benefit that consumers receive from using a good or a service after subtracting the price they paid. (See figure 7.1.) The demand curve is downward sloping, and the shaded area below

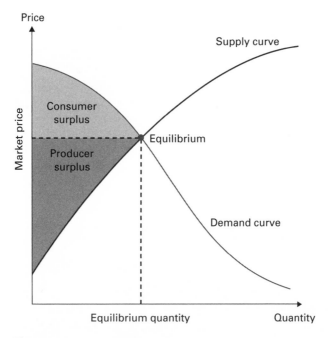

Figure 7.1
Traditional welfare analysis of a good or a service. Source: Wikipedia.

the demand curve but above the equilibrium market price represents consumer surplus. The shaded area above the supply curve and below the equilibrium market price represents profits (producer surplus), and the area below this portion of the supply curve represents the cumulative costs of production. The total revenues from the sale of a good or a service are represented by the rectangle created when the market price is multiplied by the equilibrium quantity.[5] This rectangle is what the National Income and Product Accounts do measure relatively well. Prices, quantities, and costs of goods are all obtained by the Census Bureau on a regular basis.

Although the concept of consumer surplus has been in use for quite a while, the empirical literature on how consumer surplus is used to value new products to consumers is relatively small—but it is growing.

Hausman (1997a), using the concept of consumer surplus and citing the pioneering theories of Hicks (1940) and Rothbarth (1941), demonstrated that the Consumer Price Index did not fully take into account the effect of new goods. As a result, although there have been attempts to address this critique, the CPI can significantly overstate the true rate of inflation in areas where innovation is rapid.

The Uncounted Value of Consumer Surplus

Consider how life has been transformed by air conditioning. As Gordon (2004) noted, "it has been said that the most important economic development in Asia in the twentieth century was the invention of air conditioning" (p. 124). Yet when Nordhaus (1997) examined how the CPI handled some of the major innovations of the twentieth century, he noted that when it comes to air conditioning, "outside of refrigerated transportation and productivity increases in the workplace, amenities and health effects [are] not captured in price indexes" (p. 57). Oi (1997) performed a careful analysis of the economic effects of air conditioning in the southern United States and found large increases in productivity and life expectancy because air conditioning transformed the economy there. These effects are not directly measured in GDP.

Researchers and experienced shoppers know that prices, on average, are lower on the Internet than in physical stores. Yet recent research indicates that far more of the value that the Internet provides comes from offering greater variety and choice—not just lower prices. In the first empirical paper to estimate the consumer surplus from product variety online, Brynjolfsson, Smith, and Hu (2003) showed that in the online book market consumers placed a value on variety of as much as $1 billion, which was 7–10 times as much as they valued the lower prices they found online.

Brynjolfsson (1996) used four different methods to measure the annual contribution of consumer surplus due to computers (including peripherals). He estimated that in 1987 computers generated between $50 billion and $70 billion of consumer surplus. (In 1987 the entire stock of computers in the United States was only $76 billion.) With the growth in computer capital stock, the surplus is undoubtedly much higher today.

Several studies have demonstrated the large and hidden value of consumer surplus in the economy. Bapna, Jank, and Shmueli (2008) estimated the value of consumer surplus from transactions on eBay and found that the median consumer surplus was at least $4 per auction, and that the estimated total consumer surplus was about $7 billion in 2003. None of this surplus showed up in any official statistics. For comparison, eBay's total value added was about $1 billion in 2003—this is what would show up in GDP.[6] Goolsbee and Petrin (2004) estimated consumer surplus from the introduction of Direct Broadcast Satellite service to be as large as $7 billion a year. This amount was the sum of benefits to both the satellite users and the cable users who didn't adopt DBS but still benefited from the resulting lower prices and higher-quality cable service. Ghose, Smith, and Telang (2006) used the concept of consumer surplus to demonstrate that most used-book sales on Amazon do not cannibalize the sales of new books, and that the consumer welfare gain from Amazon's used-book markets was about $67 million per year. Hausman and Leonard (2002) found that half of the welfare effects of introducing new competition in the bath tissue market accrued from product variety (the other half was from lower prices). Hausman (1997b), using consumer surplus calculations, found that the ten-year regulatory delay in introducing cell phones cost consumers $100 billion. Because these were hidden costs, they didn't appear on any income statements as "losses"—rather, the costs of the delay were calculated from the lost opportunity for benefits—and were not taken into account when considering regulation. Athey and Stern (2002) examined the value of adopting new 911 call center technologies in Pennsylvania, using innovative metrics to measure successful technological adoption. Rather than looking only at the number of ambulance trips or the time it takes to respond to an emergency, Athey and Stern undertook a detailed examination of patient health outcomes in hospitals and calculated a significant increase in total social welfare from adoption of the new technology.

Summary

Consumer surplus helps us measure the value of the introduction of new goods in a way that traditional economic measures of output and input do not. If we used consumer surplus data to examine the effects of technological innovation over the decades, we would find hundreds of billions, perhaps trillions of dollars of unmeasured benefits in the economy.

Information provides an opportunity for entirely new business models because it is costless to reproduce, unlike virtually any other good. Consider this quotation:

Thanks to Gillette, the idea that you can make money by giving something away is no longer radical. But until recently, practically everything "free" was really just the result of what economists would call a cross-subsidy: You'd get one thing free if you bought another, or you'd get a product free only if you paid for a service.

Over the past decade, however, a different sort of free has emerged. The new model is based not on cross-subsidies—the shifting of costs from one product to another—but on the fact that the cost of products *themselves* is falling fast. It's as if the price of steel had dropped so close to zero that King Gillette could give away both razor and blade, and make his money on something else entirely. (Shaving cream?) (Anderson 2008)

Developing systematic approaches to estimating this value is increasingly important as more and more of the real value of the economy is affected by information goods.

Further Reading

Chris Anderson, "Free! Why $0.00 Is the Future of Business," *Wired*, February 2008. A description of several business models that rely on free goods.

Susan Athey and Scott Stern, "The Impact of Information Technology on Emergency Health Care Outcomes," *RAND Journal of Economics* 33 (2002), no. 3: 399–432. Analyzes how the introduction of Enhanced 911 systems in Pennsylvania led to lower mortality rates and lower hospital costs, in addition to speeding up response times.

Erik Brynjolfsson, "The Contribution of Information Technology to Consumer Welfare," *Information Systems Research* 7 (1996), no. 3: 281–300. Quantifies the consumer surplus from cheaper computing due to Moore's Law and shows that it vastly exceeds the direct expenditures.

Erik Brynjolfsson, Yu (Jeffrey) Hu, and Michael Smith, "Consumer Surplus in the Digital Economy: Estimating the Value of Increased Product Variety at Online Booksellers," *Management Science* 49 (2003), no. 11: 1580–1596. Empirically demonstrates that when it comes to online shopping it is increased variety, not lower prices, that benefits consumers most.

Anindya Ghose, Michael Smith, and Rahul Telang, "Internet Exchanges for Used Books: An Empirical Analysis of Product Cannibalization and Welfare Impact," *Information Systems Research* 17 (2006), no. 1: 3–19. Studies the market for used books on Amazon and finds that used books do not cannibalize the sale of new books but rather increase consumer welfare.

8 Frontier Research Opportunities

As the economy evolves, research opportunities emerge, alternative measurement strategies gain traction, and we find better methods of identifying, measuring, and understanding how value is created. In this chapter we highlight some promising areas for future research:

• the use of task-level data (including social network analysis)

• new goods and consumer surplus measurement

• understanding organizational capital and other intangibles

• incentives for innovation in information goods and open source economics.

Research in these areas will aid managers, policy makers, and scholars in understanding how information technology, new business practices, intangible organizational investments, and innovation can lead to higher profits, economic growth, and a greater standard of living.

Task-Level Data and Social Network Analysis

Over 300 years ago, Antonie van Leeuwenhoek used a microscope to observe individual microbes (he called them "animalcules") in a drop of water and individual red corpuscles in human blood. Biology and medicine have never been the same. Today, one of the biggest opportunities for both researchers and managers is the ability to collect extremely detailed data to observe the flows of individual bits of information inside of organizations. For example, by using data from email systems and related technologies, we can track the way individuals gather and disseminate information and make decisions. These messages are routinely stored on servers and contain data on each message's sender, recipient(s), time sent, attachments included, and subject.

The power to gather and analyze such detailed data raises important privacy concerns. These can be handled in two ways. First, all participants should give their informed consent to the use of these data before they are collected. Second, it is possible to scramble and disguise the specific content of the messages and even to anonymize the participants while still retaining information about the structure and nature of information flows. (For details, see Aral, Brynjolfsson, and Van Alstyne 2007.)

Although researchers analyzing social networks have historically used interviews and paper records to painstakingly reconstruct contract patterns, the widespread use of electronic messaging now makes it possible to map social networks almost instantaneously and with far more precision and accuracy. In addition to email, other electronic communication (including instant messaging and telephone conversations, especially those involving Voice over Internet Protocol) can be mapped. More recently, smart "sociometric badges" have been developed that make it possible to track face-to-face communications (Wu et al. 2008). These developments provide an infrastructure that is eliminating the data constraint that hampered earlier research. We expect an explosion of similarly insightful research on social networks.

In addition to electronically recording communication flows, it is also possible to record details of the use of computers—even individual keystrokes and actions of information workers, again with their informed consent—in order to understand work patterns. For instance, the same data that help knowledge workers track their time for billing can be aggregated to show patterns of work at a law firm, or to identify successful or problematic work practices faced by employees at a call center. To gain the greatest benefit from such data, it is necessary to match it to clear performance metrics. Fortunately, the output of a surprising number of information workers is already tracked fairly carefully. For instance, Aral, Brynjolfsson, and Van Alstyne (2007) were able to match email data on executive recruiters to detailed accounting records of individual output and compensation, linking activities to performance on specific projects in specific months. Similarly, the compensation of many sales professionals, consultants, attorneys, doctors, writers, and other knowledge workers is linked to specific tasks or creating a specific output. Likewise, the output of many clerical and information workers can be carefully measured. When the output of individuals cannot be easily tracked, it may be possible to track the output of teams. Much as hockey statisticians calculate a "plus/minus" metric for each player on a team, the same can be done in information work for individuals participating in various teams. Metrics are improving all the time. Indeed, it has been our experience that many of the highest-performing companies are those that track intermediate and final output very carefully.

Over the next few years, this approach will open up the black box of organizations and will reveal principles, practices, and insights that would never have been uncovered with data aggregated at the firm level or the industry level.

Consumer Surplus

As we noted in chapter 2, many aspects of technology, such as the wealth of information that can now be freely obtained on the World Wide Web, are not priced but nonetheless generate significant benefits to society. This highlights the difference between traditional measures of output (which form the basis of gross domestic product and productivity accounting) and consumer welfare calculations. GDP is a measure of the market value of goods and services produced in the economy in a given period of time. If a million copies of the *Encyclopaedia Britannica* are produced and sold for $1,000 each, that generates hundreds of millions of dollars of GDP.[1] However, if a million users access Wikipedia instead, and Wikipedia is free, then that generates zero dollars of GDP. If the number of users grows from 1 million to 100 million or 1 billion, GDP is similarly unaffected.[2] Although GDP is unchanged, the welfare of those consumers is not. In particular, if a user would have been willing to pay $1,000, but instead pays $0 for the online encyclopedia, then that user has a welfare gain of $1,000. Other users might have had a lower (or a higher) willingness to pay, and the sum of these values is the total consumer surplus created by the new good. Similarly, by comparing the minimum price needed to produce a good or service (i.e., the cost) with the price actually received in the market place, we can calculate producer surplus. Because so many information goods are unpriced, it may make sense to rely on changes in the sum of consumer and producer surplus (which represent the total welfare gain) rather than on output and productivity as our primary measure of economic growth. Fortunately, the theory and techniques for using surplus are increasingly well understood. For example, as we stated earlier, the benefits of product variety created by online book sales have been carefully documented (Brynjolfsson, Hu, and Smith 2003), as have estimates of the overall gain from IT investments (Brynjolfsson 1996).

A research program that systematically documented the welfare effects of new products, quality improvements, increased product variety, improved timeliness, and other characteristics of the information economy would yield quantifiable evidence on how and where our economy is benefiting from technology advances in ways that have largely eluded traditional output and productivity calculations.

Organizational Capital and Other Intangibles

For some time now, we have been advocating that managers and economists treat organizational capital, such as business processes, more like traditional capital assets. As with physical capital, companies spend hundreds of billions of dollars developing and implementing new business processes, and these processes last for many years once they are installed. In terms of their cash flows, business processes are capital assets. We have recommended that investments in human and organizational capital be treated by the US government as investments instead of expenses, and we have advised the Census Bureau to begin to systematically measure these intangibles and classify the economy's stock of intangibles as *assets*. This would expand the definition of technology investment from hardware and software to also include the costs of reorganization and training.

Our estimate of the value of computer-enabled organizational assets held by US corporations as more than $1 trillion (Saunders and Brynjolfsson 2008), based on 2003–2006 data, is far more than the direct value of hardware or software in the US economy. The difficulty, of course, is that intangibles such as organizational capital generally do not appear in standard public or private data sets and have not been systematically measured. However, this is not to say that they are unmeasurable. Through surveys, interviews, and proxy measures, it is possible to construct estimates of organizational capital. Brynjolfsson and Hitt (2002) found that successful IT users disproportionately adopted seven practices of the "Digital Organization": technology use, decision rights, incentive systems, information flows, hiring practices, training investments, and business strategy. These could be combined to create an index of organizational capital that behaves much like other capital assets. For instance, firms with higher levels of this measure of organizational capital produce more output (with other inputs held constant). Similarly, the capital markets assign higher values to firms with more organizational capital, just as they value firms with other assets more highly.

We admit that even the best surveys and measures are just proxies, and that to truly understand every firm's unique and important organizational design would be just about impossible. As with any incomplete measure, there are going to be flaws and false positives. However, until now statistical agencies and most economists have assumed the value of this intangible capital to be zero, which we are sure is not the case. Future research has the potential to more precisely assess the nature and effects of organizational capital. Specific practices can be documented, and their financial value (or lack thereof) can be measured, using these techniques. In most cases, organizational capital would be expected to vary systematically by industry and by other aspects of the firm's environment and situation. Because it is difficult to manage what one doesn't measure, this type of research has the potential not only to improve management performance but also to speed the dissemination of successful clusters of practices.

Incentives for Innovation in Information Goods and Open Source Economics

Designing incentive mechanisms for encouraging innovation for information goods is another emerging research area. The traditional market price system works effectively for most products by providing incentives for their creation while rationing their consumption to those who have the highest values for the goods or services. However, this system has important weaknesses when applied to digital information goods. These goods may have a substantial cost for the first copy but virtually zero additional cost for all subsequent copies. The textbook rule that efficiency calls for a price equal to marginal cost would imply zero price and thus zero incentives for the creation of the first copy. This is the classic "public goods" problem. Positive prices, often enforced with digital rights systems, legal penalties, or both, will generate revenues and incentives for the creation of new goods, but at the expense of limiting access to the good, even though after the first copy it would be costless to provide universal access (which is not the case for physical goods). This has created conflicts and inefficiencies in the distribution of music, software, and (increasingly) other types of digital goods.

However, technology might also make it possible to design and implement alternative mechanisms that differ from traditional markets. In some cases, it appears possible to design allocation systems that will provide incentives for innovation that will be at least as strong as those provided by the traditional price system, and that will provide widespread, if not quite universal, access to information. (See, e.g., Brynjolfsson and Zhang 2007.) Similarly, research into the theory and practice of mechanism design that uses reputation systems and decentralized voting systems, although still in its earliest stages, holds promise for important breakthroughs. The success of eBay demonstrates the enormous value that can be unleashed when technology and rules are combined in the right way to create a marketplace. In view of the importance of innovation for economic growth, improving incentives for the creation of information and knowledge will have a tremendous payoff for the economy.

Related research looks at how open source projects, wikis, and related user-created-content efforts are structured and succeed. Both the deep coordination of Linux and the shallower coordination of Amazon ratings and reviews demonstrate how large numbers of individuals can work together in new ways. Traditional hierarchical management is not necessarily required, and even traditional market incentives aren't necessarily involved in many of these projects. Technology has enabled us to coordinate and amplify the collective intelligence of thousands, millions, and perhaps someday billions of minds to achieve goals that would otherwise be impossible. Understanding the motivations, psychology, economics, and management of these emerging systems is a very promising research area.

Concluding Thoughts

Of course, the list above is far from exhaustive. There are many other potential research questions that will surely yield important results. For instance:

- How does leadership affect innovation?
- What are the relationships among innovation, IT, and productivity?

• How can we value knowledge?

• What types of labor will be replaced by machines, and what types of labor will be in greater demand?

• How will continuing advances in IT affect the distribution of wealth? What are the security and privacy implications of ubiquitous IT?

• How will the roles of government and business change in an information economy?

• How do measures of consumer surplus influence the Consumer Price Index and outcomes of monetary policy?

One prediction that is easy to make is that the underlying technologies will continue to advance at an exponentially increasing pace for at least 10 years. Just within the next 5 years or so, the computing, communications, and data-storage power of our machines will double, redouble, and then double again. As a result, the most important limits we face will not be technological. Instead, the bottleneck will be our ability to understand how to use the technology, and thus the highest returns will go to those who are best able to widen that bottleneck.

Further Reading

Sinan Aral, Erik Brynjolfsson, and Marshall Van Alstyne, *Productivity Effects of Information Diffusion in Networks*, NBER Working Paper 13172, 2007. Data on email traffic are used to determine and study how various patterns of information diffusion affect the productivity and the performance of information workers.

Lynn Wu, Ben Waber, Sinan Aral, Erik Brynjolfsson, and Alex Pentland, "Mining Face-to-Face Interaction Networks Using Sociometric Badges: Predicting Productivity in an IT Configuration Task," *Proceedings of the International Conference on Information Systems 2008*. Sociometric badges are used to record a novel set of data to analyze face-to-face networks.

Notes

Chapter 1

1. Louis D. Johnston and Samuel H. Williamson, "What Was the U.S. GDP Then?" (2008), available at http://www.measuringworth.org.

2. Bureau of Economic Analysis, National Income and Product Accounts, "Selected Per Capita Product and Income Series in Current and Chained Dollars," table 7.1, line 1, 2008.

3. Bureau of Labor Statistics, CPI, U.S. City Average, Eggs, Grade A, Large, price per dozen, December 2008.

4. National Automobile Dealers Association, Monthly Sales Trends, *AutoExec*, March 2009, p. 24. Available at http://www.nada.org. Refers to the average 2008 price.

5. The US city average CPI for 1913 was 9.9, and in 2008 it was 215.303, reflecting an increase of 21.7 times. (The "base year" is 1982–84 = 100.)

6. Multi-factor productivity (MFP) is a much broader measure of productivity than labor productivity (output per hour worked). MFP is output divided by a wide variety of inputs, including labor, capital, energy, materials, and purchased services.

7. In this simplified example, we assume that the hours worked per person are constant, so the long-term increase in hours worked will come primarily from population growth.

8. We define an IT-using industry as any non-IT-producing industry, thus excluding industries that produce semiconductors or software.

Chapter 2

1. We calculate this by taking the ratio of 68.2/18.9, which is approximately 3.61.

2. Official GDP statistics are available from 1947 on, so we can't say definitively how far back this trend goes.

3. ICT: information and communication technologies.

4. "ICT" refers to a somewhat larger category of products and services than "IT," but in this book most of the economic insights we discuss for one also apply to the other.

5. These industries were classified by PricewaterhouseCoopers and the National Venture Capital Association, not by the Bureau of Economic Analysis, so there will be some slight differences. We grouped industries as defined by PricewaterhouseCoopers to get as close to the BEA's groupings for information industries and ICT investments as we could get in order to make a fair comparison between innovation and these industries' shares of the economy.

6. Some nonmarket goods and services are included in GDP, however. According to the BEA (2007, p. 2), they include "the defense services provided by the Federal Government, the education services provided by local governments, the emergency housing or health care services provided by nonprofit institutions serving households (such as the Red Cross), and the housing services provided by and for persons who own and live in their own home (referred to as 'owner-occupants')."

7. Goods and services are counted in GDP in the year that they are produced.

8. Neilsen NetRatings, data as of April 2009.

9. See CNET's "Download Hall of Fame" at http://www.download .com. Winamp has 77 million users (http://blog.winamp.com).

Quicktime Version 6 has been downloaded 350 million times (http://www.apple.com). ICQ has been downloaded more than 430 million times from download.com.

10. See table 7.12 in the National Income and Products Accounts data.

11. The BEA (2007, p. 5) describes why owner-occupied housing services are imputed in GDP. When one rents a house or an apartment, this market transaction is included in GDP. However, people who live in their own home do not pay rent, of course, so there is no market transaction to record. If GDP only included the rental transactions but not the owner-occupied homes, then GDP would change if a owner-occupied home became rented, or vice-versa. To prevent this from happening, the National Income and Product Accounts treat owner-occupants as though they "rent" the homes to themselves, based on market rates for similar rental properties.

12. It was called the Cost of Living Index before being renamed the Consumer Price Index in 1945.

13. It was removed twice in the early twentieth century but was restored both times.

14. According to Dow Jones: "At any given time, The Dow's 30 components usually account for 25% to 30% of the total market value of all U.S. stocks. The Dow doesn't literally "represent" the entire U.S. market. Rather, it is a blue-chip index representing the leading companies in the industries driving the U.S. stock market. As a result, its performance is highly correlated with that of indexes containing hundreds or thousands of stocks. Component changes are rare and usually occur only when an existing company is going through a major change, such as a shift in its main line of business, acquisition by another company, or bankruptcy. There is no review schedule. Changes are made as needed at the discretion of the managing editor of the *Wall Street Journal*. While the responsibility rests with this individual, other senior editors may be consulted. Selected components are always U.S. companies, are leaders in their industries, are widely held by investors, and have long records of sustained growth."

Chapter 3

1. The following equation holds when something grows at a rate of x percent for y periods and doubles: $(1 + x)^y = 2$. Taking the natural logarithm of both sides leads to $y \ln(1 + x) = \ln 2 = 0.693$. For small x, $\ln(1 + x) \approx x$, so $xy = 0.693 \approx 0.70$.

2. This is the case even though productivity in the United States fell sharply from 2004 to 2006.

Chapter 4

1. Brynjolfsson and Milgrom (2010) recently reviewed the economics of complementarities in organizations and provide an extensive literature review for readers interested in learning more about this topic. In the next few pages, we draw heavily on that work as we summarize some of the leading empirical findings and insights.

2. Milgrom and Roberts note that the 1975 Harvard Business School case detailing the company's unique business methods and compensation scheme is among the school's best-selling cases ever and is still widely taught today.

3. In practice, a host of econometric issues can obscure one or both of these tests of complementarities. For instance, it is quite possible for two practices to be correlated even if they are not complementary. For similar reasons, performance can be a misleading guide to complementarities. Essential reading for anyone contemplating a serious statistical assessment of complementarities is Athey and Stern's 1998 paper, in which they formally analyze a broad set of potential econometric problems and their potential solutions.

4. Bresnahan, Brynjolfsson, and Hitt (2002, p. 340) define skill-biased technical change as "technical progress that shifts demand toward more highly skilled workers relative to the less skilled."

5. We explore the term *organizational capital* in detail in chapter 5.

Chapter 5

1. Corrado et al. aggregate economic competencies from two sources: brand equity (such as advertising) and firm-specific resources (such as training and organizational change).

Chapter 6

1. Neilsen NetRatings, data as of April 2009.

2. Liebowitz used citation data as a proxy for number of photocopies.

Chapter 7

1. For an estimate of the number of telephones, see *Statistical Abstract of the United States*, 1917, p. 294. For the Census Bureau's estimate of the population, see http://www.census.gov.

2. *Statistical Abstract of the United States*, 1915, p. 260.

3. For an estimate of the number of registered vehicles, see *Statistical Abstract of the United States*, 1917, p. 294. We extrapolate 1913's estimate from 1914's.

4. For the 2007 estimate of motor vehicles, see http://www.fhwa.dot .gov.

5. In other words, it is the rectangle with corners at the origin, the market price, the equilibrium price, and the equilibrium quantity.

6. GDP is a measure of value added, which is total sales minus the cost of intermediate inputs, such as raw materials, energy, and purchased services. Whereas eBay's sales in 2003 were $2.16 billion, the cost of their materials its intermediate inputs was about $1 billion. The difference is a value added of $1.12 billion.

Chapter 8

1. The actual amount added to GDP would be total sales ($1 billion) minus the cost of intermediate inputs.

2. At least, it is not directly affected. Conceivably, the access to the information may affect the output of other products. Information could act as a complement to other products, spurring their sales and increasing GDP. Or, it could be a substitute for other products, reducing their sales and lowering GDP.

Bibliography

Abraham, Katharine, and Christopher Mackie. 2006. A Framework for Nonmarket Accounting. In *A New Architecture for the U.S. National Accounts*, ed. D. Jorgenson et al. University of Chicago Press.

Acemoglu, Daron, Philippe Aghion, Claire Lelarge, John Van Reenen, and Fabrizio Zilibotti. 2007. Technology, Information, and the Decentralization of the Firm. *Quarterly Journal of Economics* 122, no. 4: 1759–1799.

Aizcorbe, Ana, Carol Moylan, and Carol Robbins. 2009. Toward Better Measurement of Innovation and Intangibles. *Survey of Current Business* 89, no. 1: 10–23.

Anderson, Chris. 2008. Free! Why $0.00 Is the Future of Business. *Wired*, February.

Aral, Sinan, Erik Brynjolfsson, and Marshall Van Alstyne. 2007. Productivity Effects of Information Diffusion in Networks. Working paper 13172, National Bureau of Economic Research.

Aral, Sinan, Erik Brynjolfsson, and Marshall Van Alstyne. 2008. Information, Technology and Information Worker Productivity. Available at http://ssrn.com.

Athey, Susan, and Scott Stern. 1998. An Empirical Framework for Testing Theories About Complementarity in Organizational Design. Working paper 6600, National Bureau of Economic Research.

Athey, Susan, and Scott Stern. 2002. The Impact of Information Technology on Emergency Health Care Outcomes. *RAND Journal of Economics* 33, no. 3: 399–432.

Atkeson, Andrew, and Patrick Kehoe. 2005. Modeling and Measuring Organization Capital. *Journal of Political Economy* 113, no. 5: 1026–1053.

Autor, David, Frank Levy, and Richard Murnane. 2002. Upstairs, Downstairs: Computers and Skills on Two Floors of a Large Bank. *Industrial & Labor Relations Review* 55, no. 3: 432–447.

Autor, David, Frank Levy, and Richard Murnane. 2003. The Skill Content of Recent Technological Change: An Empirical Exploration. *Quarterly Journal of Economics* 118, no. 4: 1279–1333.

Bakos, Yannis, and Erik Brynjolfsson. 1999. Bundling Information Goods: Pricing, Profits, and Efficiency. *Management Science* 45, no. 12: 1613–1630.

Bakos, Yannis, and Erik Brynjolfsson. 2000. Bundling and Competition on the Internet. *Marketing Science* 19, no. 1: 63–82.

Bapna, Ravi, Wolfgang Jank, and Galit Shmueli. 2008. Consumer Surplus in Online Auctions. *Information Systems Research* 19, no. 4: 400–416.

Barley, Steven. 1986. Technology as an Occasion for Structuring: Evidence from Observations of CT Scanners and the Social Order of Radiology Departments. *Administrative Science Quarterly* 31, no. 1: 78–108.

Bartel, Ann, Casey Ichniowski, and Kathryn Shaw. 2007. How Does Information Technology Affect Productivity? Plant-Level Comparisons of Product Innovation, Process Improvement, and Worker Skills. *Quarterly Journal of Economics* 122, no. 4: 1721–1758.

Basu, Susanto, John Fernald, Nicholas Oulton, and Sylaja Srinivasan. 2003. The Case of the Missing Productivity Growth, or Does Information Technology Explain Why Productivity Accelerated in the United States but Not in the United Kingdom? In *NBER Macroeconomics Annual 2003*, ed. M. Gertler and K. Rogoff. MIT Press.

Berg, Norman, and Norman Fast. 1975. Lincoln Electric Co. Case 9-376-028, Harvard Business School.

Berndt, Ernst, and Catherine Morrison. 1995. High-Tech Capital Formation and Economic Performance in U.S. Manufacturing Industries: An Exploratory Analysis. *Journal of Econometrics* 65, no. 1: 9–43.

Black, Sandra, and Lisa Lynch. 2001. How to Compete: The Impact of Workplace Practices and Information Technology on Productivity. *Review of Economics and Statistics* 83, no. 3: 434–445.

Black, Sandra, and Lisa Lynch. 2004. What's Driving the New Economy?: The Benefits of Workplace Innovation. *Economic Journal* 114, no. 493: F97–F116.

Black, Sandra, and Lisa Lynch. 2005. Measuring Organizational Capital in the New Economy. In *Measuring Capital in the New Economy*, ed. C. Corrado et al. University of Chicago Press.

Bloom, Nicholas, Raffaella Sadun, and John Van Reenen. 2007. Americans Do I.T. Better: US Multinationals and the Productivity Miracle. Working Paper 13085, National Bureau of Economic Research.

Boskin, Michael, Ellen Dulberger, Robert Gordon, Zvi Griliches, and Dale Jorgenson. 1996. Toward a More Accurate Measure of the Cost of Living: Final Report to the Senate Finance Committee from the Advisory Commission to Study the Consumer Price Index. Available at http://www.ssa.gov.

Bresnahan, Timothy. 2002. Prospects for an Information-Technology-Led Productivity Surge. In *Innovation Policy and the Economy*, volume 2, ed. A. Jaffe et al. MIT Press.

Bresnahan, Timothy, Erik Brynjolfsson, and Lorin Hitt. 2002. Information Technology, Workplace Organization, and the Demand for Skilled Labor: Firm-Level Evidence. *Quarterly Journal of Economics* 117, no. 1: 339–376.

Bresnahan, Timothy, and M. Trajtenberg. 1995. General Purpose Technologies "Engines of Growth"? *Journal of Econometrics* 65, no. 1: 83–108.

Brynjolfsson, Erik. 1993. The Productivity Paradox of Information Technology. *Communications of the ACM* 36, no. 12: 67–77.

Brynjolfsson, Erik. 1996. The Contribution of Information Technology to Consumer Welfare. *Information Systems Research* 7, no. 3: 281–300.

Brynjolfsson, Erik. 2005. Seven Pillars of IT Productivity. *Optimize*, May.

Brynjolfsson, Erik, David Fitoussi, and Lorin Hitt. 2006. The Information Technology Iceberg. Working paper, MIT.

Brynjolfsson, Erik, and Lorin Hitt 2000. Beyond Computation: Information Technology, Organizational Transformation and Business Performance. *Journal of Economic Perspectives* 14, no. 4: 23–48.

Brynjolfsson, Erik, and Lorin Hitt. 2002. Digital Organization: The Seven Habits of Highly Productive Companies. Working paper, MIT.

Brynjolfsson, Erik, and Lorin Hitt. 2003. Computing Productivity: Firm-Level Evidence. *Review of Economics & Statistics* 85, no. 4: 793–808.

Brynjolfsson, Erik, Lorin Hitt, and Shinkyu Yang. 2002. Intangible Assets: Computers and Organizational Capital. *Brookings Papers on Economic Activity* 2002, no. 1: 137–198.

Brynjolfsson, Erik, Yu (Jeffrey) Hu, and Michael Smith. 2003. Consumer Surplus in the Digital Economy: Estimating the Value of Increased Product Variety at Online Booksellers. *Management Science* 49, no. 11: 1580–1596.

Brynjolfsson, Erik, Thomas Malone, Vijay Gurbaxani, and Ajit Kambil. 1994. Does Information Technology Lead to Smaller Firms? *Management Science* 40, no. 12: 1628–1644.

Brynjolfsson, Erik, Andrew McAfee, Michael Sorell, and Feng Zhu. 2009. Scale without Mass: Business Process Replication and Industry Dynamics. Working paper, MIT.

Brynjolfsson, Erik, and Paul Milgrom. 2010. Complementarity in Organizations. In *Handbook of Organizational Economics*, ed. R. Gibbons and J. Roberts. Princeton University Press.

Brynjolfsson, Erik, Amy Austin Renshaw, and Marshall Van Alstyne. 1997. The Matrix of Change. *Sloan Management Review* 38, no. 2: 37–54.

Brynjolfsson, Erik, and Michael Smith. 2000. Frictionless Commerce? A Comparison of Internet and Conventional Retailers. *Management Science* 46, no. 4: 563–585.

Brynjolfsson, Erik, and Shinkyu Yang. 1996. Information Technology and Productivity: A Review of the Literature. In *Advances in Computers*, volume 43, ed. M. Zelkowitz. Academic.

Brynjolfsson, Erik, and Xiaoquan (Michael) Zhang. 2007. Innovation Incentives for Information Goods. In *Innovation Policy and the Economy*, volume 7, ed. A. Jaffe et al. MIT Press.

Bugamelli, Matteo, and Patrizio Pagano. 2004. Barriers to Investment in ICT. *Applied Economics* 36, no. 20: 2275–2286.

Bureau of Economic Analysis. 2007. *Measuring the Economy: A Primer on GDP and the National Income and Product Accounts.* Available at http://www.bea.gov.

Bureau of Labor Statistics. 1920. Retail Prices of Food in the United States. *Monthly Labor Review* 10, no. 1: 69–89.

Bureau of Labor Statistics. 2008. How BLS Measures Price Change for Personal Computers and Peripheral Equipment in the Consumer Price Index. Available at http://www.bls.gov.

Cameron, Gavin. 1998. Innovation and Growth: A Survey of the Empirical Evidence. Mimeo, Nuffield College, Oxford.

Caroli, Eve, and John Van Reenen. 2001. Skill-Biased Organizational Change? Evidence from a Panel of British and French Establishments. *Quarterly Journal of Economics* 116, no. 4: 1449–1492.

Carr, Nicholas. 2003. IT Doesn't Matter. *Harvard Business Review* 81, no. 5: 41–49.

Chevalier, Judith, and Austan Goolsbee. 2003. Measuring Prices and Price Competition Online: Amazon.com and BarnesandNoble.com. *Quantitative Marketing and Economics* 1, no. 2: 203–222.

Colecchia, Alessandra, and Paul Schreyer. 2002. ICT Investment and Economic Growth in the 1990s: Is the United States a Unique Case? A Comparative Study of Nine OECD Countries. *Review of Economic Dynamics* 5, no. 2: 408–442.

Coase, R. 1937. The Nature of the Firm. *Economica* 4, no. 16: 386–405.

Colombo, Massimo, and Marco Delmastro. 2004. Delegation of Authority in Business Organizations: An Empirical Test. *Journal of Industrial Economics* 52, no. 1: 53–80.

Corrado, Carol, Charles Hulten, and Daniel Sichel. 2005. Measuring Capital and Technology: An Expanded Framework. In *Measuring Capital in the New Economy*, ed. C. Corrado et al. University of Chicago Press.

Corrado, Carol, Charles Hulten, and Daniel Sichel. 2006. Intangible Capital and Economic Growth. Working paper 2006–24, Finance and Economics Discussion Series, Divisions of Research & Statistics and Monetary Affairs, Federal Reserve Board, Washington.

Council of Economic Advisers. 2004. *Economic Report of the President.* Government Printing Office.

Council of Economic Advisers. 2006. *Economic Report of the President.* Government Printing Office.

Council of Economic Advisers. 2007. *Economic Report of the President.* Government Printing Office.

Crespi, Gustavo, Chiara Criscuolo, and Jonathan Haskel. 2007. Information Technology, Organisational Change and Productivity Growth: Evidence from UK Firms. Discussion paper 783, Centre for Economic Performance.

Cummins, Jason. 2005. A New Approach to the Valuation of Organizational Capital. In *Measuring Capital in the New Economy*, ed. C. Corrado et al. University of Chicago Press.

David, Paul. 1990. The Dynamo and the Computer: An Historical Perspective on the Modern Productivity Paradox. *American Economic Review* 80, no. 2: 355–361.

David, Paul, and Gavin Wright. 2003. General Purpose Technologies and Surges in Productivity: Historical Reflections on the Future of the ICT Revolution. In *The Economic Future in Historical Perspective*, ed. P. David and M. Thomas. Oxford University Press.

Dedrick, Jason, Vijay Gurbaxani, and Kenneth Kraemer. 2003. Information Technology and Economic Performance: A Critical Review of the Empirical Evidence. *ACM Computing Surveys* 35, no. 1: 1–28.

Dewan, Sanjeev and Kenneth Kraemer. 2000. Information Technology and Productivity: Evidence from Country-Level Data. *Management Science* 46, no. 4: 548–562.

Dierickx, Ingemar, and Karel Cool. 1989. Asset Stock Accumulation and Sustainability of Competitive Advantage. *Management Science* 35, no. 12: 1504–1511.

Ernst & Young. 1998. *Accounting for the Costs of Computer Software Developed or Obtained for Internal Use: Statement of Position 98-1.*

Fernald, John, and Shanthi Ramnath. 2004. The Acceleration in U.S. Total Factor Productivity after 1995: The Role of Information Technology. *Federal Reserve Bank of Chicago Economic Perspectives* 28, no. 1: 52–67.

Ghose, Anindya, Michael Smith, and Rahul Telang. 2006. Internet Exchanges for Used Books: An Empirical Analysis of Product Cannibalization and Welfare Impact. *Information Systems Research* 17, no. 1: 3–19.

Gibbons, Robert. 2005. Four Formal(izable) Theories of the Firm? *Journal of Economic Behavior & Organization* 58, no. 2: 200–245.

Goolsbee, Austan, and Peter Klenow. 2006. Valuing Consumer Products by the Time Spent Using Them: An Application to the Internet. *American Economic Review* 96, no. 2: 108–113.

Goolsbee, Austan, and Amil Petrin. 2004. The Consumer Gains from Direct Broadcast Satellites and the Competition with Cable TV. *Econometrica* 72, no. 2: 351–381.

Gordon, Robert. 2003. Exploding Productivity Growth: Context, Causes, and Implications. *Brookings Papers on Economic Activity* 2003, no. 2: 207–279.

Gordon, Robert. 2004. Five Puzzles in the Behavior of Productivity, Investment, and Innovation. In *The Global Competitiveness Report 2003–04*, ed. M. Porter et al. Oxford University Press.

Gordon, Robert. 2006. The Boskin Commission Report: A Retrospective One Decade Later. *International Productivity Monitor* 1, no. 12: 7–22.

Gormley, J., W. Bluestein, J. Gatoff, and H. Chun. 1998. The Runaway Costs of Packaged Applications. *Forrester Report* 3, no. 5: 1–15.

Greenlees, John, and Robert McClelland. 2008. Addressing Misconceptions About the Consumer Price Index. *Monthly Labor Review* 131, no. 8: 3–19.

Griliches, Zvi. 1958. Research Costs and Social Returns: Hybrid Corn and Related Innovations. *Journal of Political Economy* 66, no. 5: 419–431.

Hammer, Michael. 1990. Reengineering Work: Don't Automate, Obliterate. *Harvard Business Review* 68, no. 4: 104–112.

Hausman, Jerry. 1997a. Valuation of New Goods under Perfect and Imperfect Competition. In *The Economics of New Goods*, ed. T. Bresnahan and R. Gordon. University of Chicago Press.

Hausman, Jerry. 1997b. Valuing the Effect of Regulation on New Services in Telecommunications. *Brookings Papers on Economic Activity. Microeconomics* 1997, no. 1: 1–54.

Hausman, Jerry, and Gregory Leonard. 2002. The Competitive Effects of a New Product Introduction: A Case Study. *Journal of Industrial Economics* 50, no. 3: 237–263.

Hayek, F. A. 1945. The Use of Knowledge in Society. *American Economic Review* 35, no. 4: 519–530.

Hempell, Thomas. 2006. *Computers and Productivity: How Firms Make a General Purpose Technology Work*. Physica-Verlag.

Hicks, J. 1940. The Valuation of the Social Income. *Economica* 7, no. 26: 105–124.

Ichniowski, Casey, and Kathryn Shaw. 2003. Beyond Incentive Pay: Insiders' Estimates of the Value of Complementary Human Resource Management Practices. *Journal of Economic Perspectives* 17, no. 1: 155–180.

Ichniowski, Casey, Kathryn Shaw, and Giovanna Prennushi. 1997. The Effects of Human Resource Management Practices on Productivity: A

Study of Steel Finishing Lines. *American Economic Review* 87, no. 3: 291–313.

Jaffe, Adam, Manuel Trajtenberg, and Rebecca Henderson. 1993. Geographic Localization of Knowledge Spillovers as Evidenced by Patent Citations. *Quarterly Journal of Economics* 108, no. 3: 577–598.

Jorgenson, Dale. 2001. Information Technology and the U.S. Economy. *American Economic Review* 91, no. 1: 1–32.

Jorgenson, Dale, Mun Ho, Jon Samuels, and Kevin Stiroh. 2007. Industry Origins of the American Productivity Resurgence. *Economic Systems Research* 19, no. 3: 229–252.

Jorgenson, Dale, Mun Ho, and Kevin Stiroh. 2008. A Retrospective Look at the U.S. Productivity Growth Resurgence. *Journal of Economic Perspectives* 22, no. 1: 3–24.

Jorgenson, Dale, and Kevin Stiroh. 2000. Raising the Speed Limit: U.S. Economic Growth in the Information Age. *Brookings Papers on Economic Activity* 2000, no. 1: 125–211.

Knight, Charles. 1854. *The Old Printer and the Modern Press.* John Murray.

Kurzweil, Ray. 2001. The Law of Accelerating Returns. Available at http://www.KurzweilAI.net.

Kurzweil, Ray. 2005. *The Singularity Is Near.* Viking Penguin.

Lajili, Kaouthar, and Joseph Mahoney. 2006. Revisiting Agency and Transaction Costs Theory Predictions on Vertical Financial Ownership and Contracting: Electronic Integration as an Organizational Form Choice. *Managerial and Decision Economics* 27, no. 7: 573–586.

Leavitt, Harold, and Thomas Whisler. 1958. Management in the 1980's. *Harvard Business Review* 36, no. 6: 41–48.

Lev, Baruch, and Suresh Radhakrishnan. 2005. The Valuation of Organizational Capital. In *Measuring Capital in the New Economy*, ed. C. Corrado et al. University of Chicago Press.

Liebowitz, S. 1985. Copying and Indirect Appropriability: Photocopying of Journals. *Journal of Political Economy* 93, no. 5: 945–957.

Lipsey, Richard, Cliff Bekar, and Kenneth Carlaw. 1998. What Requires Explanation. In *General Purpose Technologies and Economic Growth*, ed. E. Helpman. MIT Press.

Loveman, Gary. 1994. An Assessment of the Productivity Impact of Information Technologies. In *Information Technology and the Corporation of the 1990s: Research Studies*, ed. T. Allen and M. Morton. Oxford University Press.

Lyman, Peter, and Hal Varian. 2003. How Much Information? Available at http://www.sims.berkeley.edu.

Malone, Thomas. 2004. *The Future of Work: How the New Order of Business Will Shape Your Organization, Your Management Style, and Your Life.* Harvard Business School Press.

McKinsey Global Institute. 2001. *U.S. Productivity Growth 1995–2000: Understanding the Contribution of IT Relative to Other Factors.* Available at http://www.mckinsey.com.

Milgrom, Paul, Yingyi Qian, and John Roberts. 1991. Complementarities, Momentum, and the Evolution of Modern Manufacturing. *American Economic Review* 81, no. 2: 84–88.

Milgrom, Paul, and John Roberts. 1990. The Economics of Modern Manufacturing: Technology, Strategy, and Organization. *American Economic Review* 80, no. 3: 511–528.

Milgrom, Paul, and John Roberts. 1995. Complementarities and Fit: Strategy, Structure, and Organizational Change in Manufacturing. *Journal of Accounting and Economics* 19, no. 2–3: 179–208.

Moore, Gordon. 1965. Cramming More Components onto Integrated Circuits. *Electronics* 38, no. 8: 114–117.

Nakamura, Leonard. 2001. Investing in Intangibles: Is a Trillion Dollars Missing from GDP? *Federal Reserve Bank of Philadelphia Business Review* Q4: 27–37.

Nakamura, Leonard. 2003. A Trillion Dollars a Year in Intangible Investment and the New Economy. In *Intangible Assets: Values, Measures, and Risks*, ed. J. Hand and B. Lev. Oxford University Press.

Nalebuff, Barry. Bundling as an Entry Barrier. 2004. *Quarterly Journal of Economics* 119, no. 1: 159–187.

Nordhaus, William. 1997. Do Real-Output and Real-Wage Measures Capture Reality? The History of Light Suggests Not. In *The Economics of New Goods*, ed. T. Bresnahan and R. Gordon. University of Chicago Press.

Nordhaus, William. 2005. Irving Fisher and the Contribution of Improved Longevity to Living Standards. *American Journal of Economics and Sociology* 64, no. 1: 367–392.

Nordhaus, William. 2006. Principles of National Accounting for Nonmarket Accounts. In *A New Architecture for the U.S. National Accounts*, ed. D. Jorgenson et al. University of Chicago Press.

Nordhaus, William. 2007. Two Centuries of Productivity Growth in Computing. *Journal of Economic History* 67, no. 1: 128–159.

Nordhaus, William, and James Tobin. 1972. Is Growth Obsolete? In *Economic Growth, Fiftieth Anniversary Colloquium V*. Columbia University Press.

Oi, Walter. 1997. The Welfare Implications of Invention. In *The Economics of New Goods*, ed. T. Bresnahan and R. Gordon. University of Chicago Press.

Oliner, Stephen, and Daniel Sichel. 2000. The Resurgence of Growth in the Late 1990s: Is Information Technology the Story? *Journal of Economic Perspectives* 14, no. 4: 3–22.

Oliner, Stephen, and Daniel Sichel. 2002. Information Technology and Productivity: Where Are We Now and Where Are We Going? *Federal Reserve Bank of Atlanta Economic Review* 87, no. 3: 15–44.

Oliner, Stephen, Daniel Sichel, and Kevin Stiroh. 2007. Explaining a Productive Decade. *Brookings Papers on Economic Activity* 2007, no. 1: 81–152.

O'Mahony, Mary, and Bart van Ark, eds. 2003. *EU Productivity and Competitiveness: An Industry Perspective. Can Europe Resume the Catching-up Process?* European Commission.

Organisation for Economic Co-operation and Development. 2001. *Measuring Productivity: Measurement of Aggregate and Industry-Level Productivity Growth.* OECD.

Osterman, Paul. 1991. The Impact of IT on Jobs and Skills. In *The Corporation of the 1990s: Information Technology and Organizational Transformation*, ed. M. Morton. Oxford University Press.

Oulton, Nicholas, and Sylaja Srinivasan. 2005. Productivity Growth and the Role of ICT in the UK: An Industry View 1970–2000. Discussion Paper 681, Centre for Economic Performance.

Parker, Geoffrey, and Marshall Van Alstyne. 2005. Two-Sided Network Effects: A Theory of Information Product Design. *Management Science* 51, no. 10: 1494–1504.

Pearce, Esther. 1957. *History of the Standard Industrial Classification.* Bureau of the Budget, Executive Office of the President.

Pilat, Dirk. 2004. The ICT Productivity Paradox: Insights from Micro Data. *OECD Economic Studies* 38, no. 1: 37–65.

Porter, Michael. 1996. What Is Strategy? *Harvard Business Review* 74, no. 6: 61–78.

Reinsdorf, Marshall, and Jack Triplett. Forthcoming in 2010. A Review of Reviews: Ninety Years of Professional Thinking About the Consumer Price Index. In *Price Index Concepts and Measurement*, ed. E. Diewert et al. University of Chicago Press.

Roach, Stephen. 1987. *America's Technology Dilemma: A Profile of the Information Economy.* Morgan Stanley Special Economic Study.

Robbins, Carol, and Carol Moylan. 2007. Research and Development Satellite Account Update: Estimates for 1959–2004. *Survey of Current Business* 87, no. 10: 49–64.

Roberts, John. 2004. *The Modern Firm: Organizational Design for Performance and Growth.* Oxford University Press.

Rothbarth, E. 1941. The Measurement of Changes in Real Income under Conditions of Rationing. *Review of Economic Studies* 8, no. 2: 100–107.

Saunders, Adam, and Erik Brynjolfsson. 2008. An Asset Approach to Valuing Information. Working paper, MIT.

Shapiro, Carl, and Hal Varian. 1999. *Information Rules: A Strategic Guide to the Network Economy*. Harvard Business School Press.

Solow, Robert. 1957. Technical Change and the Aggregate Production Function. *Review of Economics and Statistics* 39, no. 3: 312–320.

Solow, Robert. 1987. We'd Better Watch Out. *New York Times Book Review*, July 12.

Stieglitz, Nils, and Klaus Heine. 2007. Innovations and the Role of Complementarities in a Strategic Theory of the Firm. *Strategic Management Journal* 28, no. 1: 1–15.

Stigler, George. 1961. The Economics of Information. *Journal of Political Economy* 69, no. 3: 213–225.

Stiroh, Kevin. 2002. Measuring Information Technology and Productivity in the New Economy. *World Economics* 3, no. 1: 43–58.

Stiroh, Kevin. 2004. Reassessing the Impact of IT on the Production Function: A Meta-Analysis and Sensitivity Tests. Working paper, Federal Reserve Bank of New York.

Stiroh, Kevin. 2009. Volatility Accounting: A Production Perspective on Increased Economic Stability. *Journal of the European Economic Association* 7, no. 4: 671–696.

Topkis, Donald. 1978. Minimizing a Submodular Function on a Lattice. *Operations Research* 26, no. 2: 305–321.

Williamson, Oliver. 1979. Transaction-Cost Economics: The Governance of Contractual Relations. *Journal of Law and Economics* 22, no. 2: 233–261.

Williamson, Oliver. 1985. *The Economic Institutions of Capitalism: Firms, Markets, Relational Contracting*. Free Press.

Williamson, Oliver. 1989. Transaction Cost Economics. In *Handbook of Industrial Organization*, volume 1, ed. R. Schmalensee and R. Willig. Elsevier.

Wu, Lynn, Ben Waber, Sinan Aral, Erik Brynjolfsson, and Alex Pentland. 2008. Mining Face-to-Face Interaction Networks Using Sociometric Badges: Predicting Productivity in an IT Configuration Task. In *Proceedings of the International Conference on Information Systems 2008.*

Yang, Shinkyu, and Erik Brynjolfsson. 2001. Intangible Assets and Growth Accounting: Evidence from Computer Investments. Paper 136, MIT Center for Digital Business.

Index